A collection of classic writing

NORFOLK

An Anthology

Eastern Daily Press

Published by Eastern Counties Newspapers, Prospect House, Rouen Road, Norwich, Norfolk, NR1 1RE.

Printed and bound by Mackays Printers and Bookbinders, Badger Road, Lordswood, Chatham, Kent, ME5 8TD.

ISBN 0-9502952-1-3

Front cover illustration by James Paton.
Produced by Peter Waters.

Contents

Facing page: *Top: The Scottish trawler, Sunlight from Peterhead, unloads its catch of herring at Yarmouth. Bottom: A 1952 photograph of the Reedham ferry.*
Overpage: *Lunch break during a hard day's labour of stacking peas and oats at West Barsham in 1955.*

A night-time study of Norwich Cathedral's Erpingham Gate, looking out to Augustine Steward's House, Tombland.

Foreword

January 1997

There have been many Norfolk anthologies published down the years, some of the best of them by writers featured in this collection. This one, however, differs from the others in so far as it reflects the not insignificant role played by the Eastern Daily Press in showcasing their talents and their enthusiasm for our county.

The EDP, through its letter columns, its news stories and its writers and columnists, is the voice of the county. It has chronicled Norfolk life for almost 130 years, and its journalists and contributers have produced a vast body of work rich in the county's heritage. We have tried to capture the essence of that glorious outpouring in this single volume.

It has not been an easy task. As far back as the mid-1930s the EDP began to include weekly essays contributed by established local writers, in which fine writing went hand in hand with a talent for reflecting the very qualities that give this county of ours its unique spirit.

All of the articles reprinted here have been taken from the pages of the EDP over the past 60 years. Many have been included in the popular Classic EDP series of articles chosen by Charles Roberts and which have become a regular feature of the newspaper since last October. To these have been added essays selected from our archives by Philip Preston, who has been largely responsible for this project's fulfilment, Peter Waters and Steve Snelling; each essay representative of the people, the landscape and the events which have helped to shape our county and our lives.

The result, we trust, is an eclectic and evocative mix of recollections and ruminations to stir the hearts of all those who take pride in living in this eastern corner of our country – from Eric Fowler's profound and prophetic musings on the old Norwich Cattle Market to Henry Williamson's enigmatic commentary on wartime farming at Stiffkey and from Ted Ellis' vivid observations on the natural world to Lilias Rider Haggard's reflections on the impact of the Black Death on rural life.

We have also stretched the parameters of the book in order to find room for Adrian Bell, one of the century's most noted writers on the countryside whose thoughts on Suffolk as a "peculiar place" demanded inclusion.

And, of course, the collection would not be complete without the addition of a selection of articles written over the past two years by Charles Roberts, whose own lyrical style is so resonant of the past masters.

Together, these essays and articles represent the very best of EDP writing over the past six decades. In their own way, they are quintessential Norfolk.

Peter Franzen
Editor
Eastern Daily Press

Gathering clouds

November 1938

Lilias Rider Haggard

Sunday, November 6th
Armistice Sunday, which this year sees a country offering its remembrance with a deep thankfulness and a growing hope that the peace so hardly won may abide with us and our sorely tried generation.

It has been a week of wonderful weather, sunny and quiet and very warm. In just such a week in October, many years ago, I first saw the battlefields of France and Belgium, then still a desert of tangled wire and shell holes, and blasted stumps that had once been trees.

Ypres re-arising from a pile of ruins, the Menin Road, Passchendaele, and all that great stretch of shell-torn salient, a bleak and barren land where man and nature daily toiled to hide the scars of war.

A country every mile of which had been fought for, bled for, died for, lost and regained countless times all through those interminable years. There still seemed no life, no colour, no sign of man's homely and natural occupations, until some sudden unexpected turn in the road showed a garden, green grass, the blaze of late summer flowers, and all things orderly and beautiful – a British cemetery, a garden in which other things grew beside flowers, thousands upon thousands of small wooden crosses, slowly being replaced by headstones, many nameless marking "one of the great company of the unknown." In each garden they also built a Cross of Remembrance, a bronze sword gleaming on its grey stone. They tower above all else, stark emblems such as all down the centuries have stood as symbols of human and divine suffering endured to the uttermost – endured, so it seemed only a little while ago, in vain.

Monday, 7th
We went up through Norfolk to the coast. Seldom if ever have I seen the country so aflame with colour.

The little mere and the woods by the old toll-gate at Westwick was a picture hard to forget.

We ran on through North Walsham, where some of my forebears lived, and my great-great-grandfather (so tradition says) rode over here for breakfast with his son. So he must have been an active old gentlemen, as it's a good 30 miles from door to door.

Through Paston, pausing to look at the great tithe barn, past Bacton Abbey – once a power in the land because it treasured a piece of the true cross – and on to Ormesby.

We stopped where the road runs across the Broad, lying still and dark under the grey November sky. The wide beds of reed have turned to brilliant gold and brown, their tasseled heads to a sheet of silver, dim yet luminous, stretching away to the horizon.

It was nearly dark as we came through the long outskirts of Yarmouth, so different a town to the Yarmouth of the past "enclosed and fortified with moat and great walls" and by innumerable bastions and towers as in the day of Manship.

Lights had sprung out of the gloom as we ran past the docks, piled high with Baltic timber, and past the long lines of snub-nosed, squat little drifters black against the darkening sky, over the flat expanse of Haddiscoe marshes, past the round-towered church lonely on its hill in the dusk, and so home.

Tuesday, 8th
Last night's eclipse was, it seems spoilt for many by cloud. Here on a night as warm as summer a full moon sailed up a perfectly clear sky and filled the whole bowl of the valley with brilliant light, until a small rounded shadow began to eat away at its eastern edge.

I sat on the river steps watching it. Everything was very quiet, only the gentle bump of the canoe below me as she swung in the almost imperceptible current, the swirl and plop of a fish rising in the pool, and the long wavering double note of an owl hunting down the side of the wood.

As the world grew gradually dark the stars, which had been paled to nothingness by the moon's brilliance, grew bright again, the smoky blur of the Pleiades, Orion striding up the south-eastern sky, and the Milky Way showed like golden grain in the north.

At last the moon was covered yet luminous, a strange orange sphere which by the loss of its radiance had gained substance and form, it floated ghostly and mystical in the sky above and in the water at my feet revealed as it really is, a world like ours, yet dead and blasted. Actually one of the smallest visible objects we can see in the heavens as night, yet to our eyes over-shadowing all the mighty suns of the universe, controlling our tides and – so scientists tell us – much else which lives and grows upon the surface of the earth.

Thursday, 10th
A mild, grey day with hardly a leaf stirring. A visitor, used to Devon and Somerset, wished to see how the Staghounds hunted carted deer, so we went over to the meet at Winfarthing.

In that flat and open country, intersected with innumerable small roads, we managed to keep up with the hunt quite easily, and had a very good morning, especially as the deer ran in two complete circles and came back practically to starting point.

G slightly astonished to behold the quarry, apparently quite unperturbed, capering among cars and followers, while enthusiastic helpers tried in vain to clasp her round the neck!

Friday, 11th
Armistice Day, and most appropriately St Martin's Day, for St Martin was a soldier saint and the patron saint of soldiers.

The son of a Roman military tribune, he was born in Hungary about 316, and himself became a soldier.

The legend is that while serving in Amiens one bitter November morning he cut his cloak in half with his sword to wrap a naked beggar lying without the gate, whereupon the sun came out and warmed the air, and every year we have St Martin's summer in remembrance of his charity.

Where are we going?

January 1939

Lilias Rider Haggard

Sunday, January 1st
Another year, not greatly regretted, has become a tale that is told. Each one of us must have had many anxious thoughts in the last 12 months as to what the future held, not only for ourselves but for the generations for which we prepare the way.

Mankind during the last century has caught at the fringes of the still almost-unguessed-at forces which control the universe. He has let loose powers which he finds it increasingly hard to hold. The power of machinery, the power of light in all its manifestation of rays which he only begins to comprehend. The power to put a girdle round the earth not in minutes but in seconds, to speak across continents and seas.

Already he is groping in space in an effort to reach beyond the universe itself. Like every achievement it exacts its price. Mankind has lost all sense of security, nothing is too amazing or too terrible to happen. The radio produces a play and says there is an invasion from Mars and America – panic-stricken – believes the incredible.

In the back of all our minds dwells the question, "Where are we going?"

It is like the old story of the magician's apprentice who knew a little of his master's lore. He drew a magic circle, repeated the magic formula – and the spell worked.

His sober everyday environment became convulsed. Within the circle danced his faithful servants the kettle, the broom, the saucepan, the gridiron and his boots. Madly they danced and madly he danced with them... on and on, for he knew no words to break the spell.

Monday, 2nd
Last night we sat and listened to the bells of Europe chiming a New Year message over half the world. Jerusalem, Rumania, Poland, England, Germany, high-pitched carillons, shrill-jangling chimes, the swing and lift of a perfect peal and the deep-throated boom of some vast bell echoing through space and striking down to where dwell the old fears of men and women; war-pestilence-famine-fire-and-flood.

For in those brazen voices lies the whole gamut of human emotion, a rhythm which beams upon the inner consciousness, a dim world which prisons the height of all joy and the depth of all sorrow. They symbolise victory and irreparable loss, life and the making of all things new – death and the ultimate end of man and the work of his hands.

Tuesday, 3rd
The sun rose this morning a great fiery ball from a bank of grey fog, throwing a scarlet bar across the flood waters which for three days have spread themselves, a placid steely expanse, across the common.

They have dropped a couple of inches, as the tops of the posts which carry the landing stage are just appearing again. Lying in bed one might imagine there was a harbour beneath the windows, for dozens of gulls are skirling and diving in the shallows, much to the perturbation of the four ducks, Martha, Matilda, Bertha and Belinda.

Heard the kingfisher this morning on his eight o'clock beat past the house, the first time for a fortnight. I was afraid he was a casualty, as both frost and flood make fishing almost impossible for men.

Wednesday, 4th

There are often discussions as to whether it is worthwhile to keep hens in a small way for a household.

This last month I have kept a record of nine Rhode Island-Black Leghorn cross pullets. I bought 10 in November, sold to me as young pullets not yet in lay. One went sick and had to be destroyed, the others, although in poor condition, starting laying within the week. In December the nine pullets laid one hundred and thirty-three eggs, and the eggs were anything up to tuppence three-farthings each.

Autumn observations

October 1942

Lilias Rider Haggard

Sunday, October 23rd
Went during the weekend to collect some pullets from Topcroft Hall. Its mistress showed me a drawing of the house as it was about 1790, with a dignified pillared Queen Anne front and two spacious side wings. The front portion was burnt down, rebuilt much more modestly, and again rebuilt about 50 years ago. Behind still remain portions of the original hall, a house of far earlier date, with great kitchens, Tudor fireplaces, and massive oak beams.

A bedroom known originally as "Court Room", with a lovely ceiling is, I should say, part of the house to which Sir Thomas Brews brought Dame Elizabeth and their daughter Marjorie from Salle in Norfolk about the year 1476, having inherited the manor with that of Denton, from his wife's brother, Sir Gilbert Debenham. It was from Topcroft Hall that Marjorie wrote the letters to her lover, John Paston, including the famous one to "her right well beloved Valentine," assuring him that though her father had forbidden the match "to do the greatest labour that any women in love might, I would not forsake you, and if ye love me as I trust verily that ye do, ye will not leave me therefor."

The course of true love ran anything but smoothly, but in the end Marjorie married her John, and in the summer of 1478 her first child, a boy, was born at Topcroft. In the garden I was shown a mulberry tree – from the appearance of the huge split trunk of very great age. The owners wonder if it stood there when Marjorie wrote her love letters to John Paston, and if she put her "fair boy Christopher" to sleep under its shade nearly 500 years ago. Pretty Marjorie, who was also "worshipful, virtuous and good" even in the eyes of her critical Paston "in-laws"!

Monday, 24th
The fourth week in October, and still the nasturtiums and dahlias sprawled and flaunted in the garden untouched by frost. On Saturday, however, the wind shifted to the eastward, giving us another day of cloudless weather. That night the frost came, leaving the lush growth blackened, limp and clammy, to be swept away by G before breakfast.

Only a bowl of golden trumpets stand on the table saved from the slaughter. From them an occasional earwig drops and scurries away, searching in frantic haste for a new abode, for now is the time earwigs set up housekeeping. She will dwell virtuously with her spouse through the autumn and early winter, but sometime after Christmas the husband will be expelled from the cranny which they are inhabiting and she will get busy laying half a hundred eggs, which are tended with great care until the babies hatch. They are never left for many weeks.

You will find the family under logs and stones, pale grey little objects undergoing one of the four moults before they are mature at about 16 weeks, and go into the world on their own. The earwig is one of those unconsidered and unappreciated children of nature who has survived for aeons. Nobody loves them, but they were here some sixty million years ago, sprung from a remote insect which was also supposed to have been the forebear of the cockroach.

Tuesday, 25th

Saw one of the two magpies last night and woe followed swiftly on the prophesy, as I descended the entire length of a very steep flight of stairs with greater speed than grace, landing with a crash on the mat at the bottom. An apprehensive household shot from their beds expecting to pick up nothing but pieces, but rather to my surprise, extensive bruises and various chips on elbows and knees were all the damage.

Another lovely day, and we took the punt and paddled up the river in the hot sunshine filled – like the cattle standing on the bank soft-eyed and ruminative – with silent content. Looking back at the woods behind the cottage one saw where the frost had touched them, turning the elms to brilliant yellow, oaks and beech to bronze, and hedge maple to fiery red.

Norfolk families

November 1942

Lilias Rider Haggard

I have often been puzzled by the frequent mention of "tanning" in old accounts and place names; every estate of any size seems to have had a tanning yard. In an old letter of my grandfather's I found the reason. The whole letter is amusing, as it is typical of his energetic personality – "allus pokin' arter somthin'," as one of his old servants once said to me. One winter day in 1884 he had arrived an hour too soon for a meeting of the Norwich Castle Prison Committee, and filled in the time writing a long screed to Colonel Bulwer, of East Dereham, upon some passages (of which he did not approve) in Jessop's introduction to Carthew's history of the Bradenhams, Necton and Holme Hale. His family and the Masons of Necton had been friends for generations, and after a long discourse on family histories he says:

"No doubt they rose from being yeomen, but what of that; I think Lord Bacon says, 'The yeomen is ore, which refined in the next generation makes the gentleman...' and as for being Tanners, what, may I ask of that? Very many of the old Norfolk families made large fortunes by tanning, they had so much wood on their estates it was an easy way of doing so; you will see it at Gressenhall, where there was a great tannery; in fact, it is still called the Tannery Farm, and was doubtless a remnant of the L'Estrange farm buildings, and no one will question their antiquity as a family of gentle blood.

"'When Adam delved, and Eve span – Who was then a Gentleman?' Was not that said of Kett the Tanner? The South American Masons carry the same arms, and that is important when arms have been carried by a family for many centuries and are not recently adopted. No doubt they came from Necton when so many younger sons emigrated from Norfolk to Virginia in the days of Queen Elizabeth.

"As you take so much interest in Norfolk antiquarian matters I tell you what I know. I look at these matters in this light – they are not unimportant – on them depend the English character, which is very remarkable in its qualities of energy and vigour. It is formed by the different races which have occupied our Island, as indeed is its political constitution. Colonel Mason used to say his family bought Necton in the reign of Henry VII, being London merchants– I should doubt it, I think they were pure Saxon in origin – your family, too, probably. The Gurdons, our neighbours, are pure Norman. I have seen their name spelt the same in Normandy; so I have that of Caley to whom, as you know, the Conqueror granted Bradenham. I have not the slightest doubt that Mr Caley of this city (from whose place I write) has a perfect claim to descent from them. My own family is pure Danish – Mr Rye says the name frequently occurs in the Rolls of Flegg Hundred, a Danish Settlement. Then we have the Boileaus, descendants of the French refugee noblesse – and many others.

"These together – this different blending of families – make England, and have made history, and that is why one regrets that they who have served her so well are dying out. In my boyish days I used to pass part of my holidays in Necton, and much friendly chat can I remember over the fire after our five o'clock dinners from the Old Squire (William

Mason, died 1835). The burden of it this, 'here we have lived, generation after generation, doing nothing in the great arena of public life – *fruges consumere nati* – rearing our families, ordering our own acres, and making way in due time for our sons.' On one occasion, looking across at his two sons asleep over the fire, he added, 'And now neither of those two fellows will get married!' which they never did, and the family came to an end in the male line."

Having finished his letter, my energetic grandparent slumped off to his Prison Committee no little grieved at the changes he saw around him. He was spared the knowledge that not one of his seven sons would hold the little estate he had cared for so conscientiously.

There was an old tradition amongst country people that, on the Eve of All Souls, the past generations of a family came back at midnight and gathered round the fire – the warm hearth which was once the centre of their household. From then until cockcrow they were permitted to sit in the place of their children, and see what they had done with their heritage, those children in whom they lived again, in the tilt of an eyebrow, the gesture of a hand, the inflection of a voice, even in the written word and the form in which it is phrased, for blood will always betray itself, and the stamp of family is very deep in its imprint, be it in hall, farm or cottage. Those generations of family ghosts, bluff, hearty, country squires, sporting parsons, and yeomen-farmers, if they still wandered back through the sad autumn night they would find many a hearth cold and house empty of their own blood. The families came to an end because they were what my father called "bred out" and left no heirs, or because agriculture had ruined them, and they were forced to sell, or they had just drifted away and vanished in the maw of the towns. Of my grandfather's friends hardly one family is left, and of those that are, war takes a daily increasing toll. The Hall, the Home Farm, the Rectory and the Dower House know them no more.

Does it matter, I wonder? Possibly like the Masons of Necton, generation after generation have done nothing in the great arena of public life, or as old Mr Mason, quoting his Horace, said, *"Nos numerus sumus et fruges consumere nati"* (We are the ciphers, fit for nothing but to eat our share of the earth's fruits). But they and their like were the heart of England, their roots went deep into the soil which they served according to their lights, and left fairly parcelled out amongst their numerous offspring, but usually so settled that the estates were not dispersed.

It was that wise old statesman, Edmund Burke, who said: "Because half a dozen grasshoppers under a fern make the field ring with their importunate chink, whilst thousands of great cattle reposed beneath the shadow of the British oak, chew the cud and are silent, pray do not imagine that those who make the noise are the only inhabitants of the field."

Seven years

December 1942

Lilias Rider Haggard

I have been writing these Country Notes for just on seven years. The early days seem a long way off now, lost in the sunshine of past summers, before the shadow of coming events started to creep slowly but steadily across the garden of our lives. The garden wherein grew some many flowers, of supposed stability, security and prosperity, which after the stormy times of the last war one liked to think (resolutely closing the mind to any other possibility) would endure for our time.

Seven years, which have seen the youngest members of the young generation of our family circle grow up from children to take their place in helping "to shape the million-handed labour to an end and outcome."

So many happy holidays down by the river; summers on the North Norfolk coast, bathing and sailing; the fishing trips by car to Wales and Scotland; the journey to Bavaria, still a fairytale country of happy-hearted people, where no hint of the vast underworld of sinister preparation was allowed to reach the warmly-welcomed visitor – all found a record in the Country Diary. Looking back at those cuttings seems almost like the tale of another life.

"What do you find to say week after week all these years?" is a question often asked, and which leaves me more often that not, in what a discerning literary friend of mine calls a "knowing silence." He, far more than I, knows the secrets of our common trade. The fact, which sounds silly explained but is still none the less the truth, is that I have had nothing in particular to say, except the little ordinary events which happen to every one of us all day and every day.

Since the war many of these have been forbidden. The snow may rise to the window sills, the pipes be frozen solid, our only means of communication the large toboggan harnessed to a puzzled but patient pony. Strange and varied objects may descend on our heads from the skies; misguided explosions on the part of our gallant defenders cause the ceilings (solid Victorian plaster three inches thick) to come down, break up the happy home, and give the unfortunate dog worse air raid nerves than any enemy effort.

Many events – comic, tragic and dramatic – may occur, but one's lips are sealed, of if they are not the blue pencil in the office deals with the matter.

Yet rather to my surprise many people write that they enjoy the Notes, and that they travel out to various battlefields across the world. For that I am more than a little grateful, for they have brought a great deal of pleasure to their parent.

I have so often felt that what I had to say was trivial and commonplace in relation to the tremendous times in which we live. The tragic disasters, the agonising cruelties, the heartrending anxieties and griefs which wrack the world and face one on every side; what have they to do with a record of the daily round in an ever narrowing domestic circle, which is the lot of most of us when the younger ones go out to war. Who cares to hear when the fields beyond the stackyard are sown and reaped, if the thrushes sing down in the wood, or the marsh harrier swings over the reed beds, the sun glinting on her mottled plumage? Who wants to know when the first primroses are in flower under the elms, or what day the cuckoo is heard shouting down the valley – in these days when for so many the golden bowl is broken and the silver cord loosed.

Strangely enough it seems that they have their place. Perhaps because they are part of the real value of life, things which will remain stable and untouched when the nightmares of man's creating have passed away. They are the natural things which make men happy, bringing peace, contentment and fulfilment. Ruskin knew this when he said, "Now and then a wearied King or a tormented slave found out where the true kingdoms of the world were, and possessed himself in a furrow or two of garden ground, of a truly infinite dominion."

Many years ago my father wrote a book, a record of little things, of the change of the seasons and the tide of agricultural life, of the birds and beasts and fruits of the earth, "which is at once our mother and monument." On the last day of the old year he finished it with a message which has always struck me as holding all we mean to say when we say from our hearts – "A Happy New Year." In wishing that to all who read this I therefore borrow it unashamed. "Now, above every time and season, in this moment when the world beneath us leaps to the pathway of another year, to Him who, with an equal hand, makes the Star and Child, and the Corn to grow, and their use fulfilled, calls back the energy of life He lent them; to the Lord of birth and death; of spring, of summer, and of harvest, let us make the offering of a thankful spirit for all that we have been spared of ill and all that we have won of good, before we rise up in quietness and confidence to meet the fortune of the days to be."

Coastal ghosts

May 1943

Henry Williamson

Once the coast here was lower, and the sea came up the channels with every tide, bearing wooden ships burthened with cargoes which were unloaded on the quays and taken inland on wagons.

Many sailed away with grain, to other ports in England, who wanted the North Norfolk barleys for beer. Gold was the medium by which payments were made, but not the paramount purpose of the exchange. The general principle was that of exchange of goods in the community.

Northumbria wanted barley to make beer to feed the coal-miners and East Anglia wanted coal. So barques with coal left Newcastle and drew into Cley and Blakeney and Overy and Burnham, and returned with barley and wheat.

The farmer sent his loaded wagon, painted with bright colours, drawn by four horses, from his black barn door to the quayside granary of his merchant, trusting him to pay the right price for the grain, and often as not the wagon came back with a load of coal or other goods.

Water was the only means of moving heavy goods over long distances, for the roads were full of holes, and many of them not properly repaired since the Romans left centuries before.

The coastal traffic of England, with the lesser movement on canals, was the chief means of trading; thus we were from the earliest times a maritime race, a little continent on our own, made up of all the adventurous elements in Europe... hardy Danes, pioneering Vikings, sturdy Icelanders, clever Phoenicians, thorough Romans, tenacious Normans.

Small wonder then that as the scope of sailing ships increased this amalgam of virile European stocks – grafted to the easy-going native Celts – know as the English, sailed to other coasts and landed there and fought or made friends with the natives and eventually, with the coming of steam, consolidated the greatest Empire in the world; and as a nation, remained undefeated and uninvaded through scores of wars during nearly a thousand years.

Whether these little familiar ports had silted up in the flow of tides, or had remained open, their trade would have declined eventually; for with the technical advance of the machine, and of industrialism with it, the old trade on the basis of exchange and mutual trust, the old honest life of craftsmanship pre-eminent as a standard of life, was superseded by competitive big business and the idea of seeking monetary profit anywhere in the world.

Counterfeit quantity succeeded quality; the old standards decayed; speculation and cunning took the place of stability and hard, productive work. These changes were gradual and came about through so many intervolved circumstances that only the clearest and strongest minds were able to see how the new idiom of profit for the sake of profit was likely to despoil the native English character.

Financial interests ruled the world and those interests came largely into cosmopolitan hands.

Usury became paramount over craftsmanship; the materialists triumphed over the artists. Much of the literature of the 19th century was disguised social criticism; and only towards the end of the century did this criticism of materialism begin to perceive that the economic system was at the base of the artists' dissatisfaction.

Later, books like John Galsworthy's Man of Property, though often sentimental at base and satirising the men and manners of dividends instead of the God Dividend, began to make it plain to the ordinary man that the chasm between spiritual hopes and materialistic reality was too great.

Whether the little ports of the Norfolk coast had silted or not, it is probable that they would have fallen into disuse, due to causes hitherto beyond control.

I write "hitherto", because today we are beginning to control, through necessity, some of those causes. And the will to alter the conditions of the causes is beginning to form itself in the minds of millions.

For myself, I rejoice to see the economy and orderliness, where before was waste and disorder; I am happy by the sight of hedges being trimmed once more and arable being cultivated, of slum children growing sturdy and natural in the countryside, of the feeling of resurgence underlying the circumstances of war, of the chastening knowledge that we were all responsible for something that was not good enough, and therefore are now aware of our attitude towards the future.

These thoughts come into my head as I cycled along the coast the other day, surveying the effects of the greatest gale of the war.

Land reclamation

November 1943

Henry Williamson

It is pleasant to walk on English land that has been "reclaimed". The other afternoon I was standing below a wood on the slope of a field.

When first I had walked over the field, seven years before to the day, it had been bleak and bare with old grey grass, from which arose thin black thistles and tiny brown stems of seeded docks. Rabbit burrows were marked in the wet expanse of heaps of chalk and scratchings in the yellow soil.

It was a dreary scene on that November day of 1936. The three gateways of the sloping field were almost closed by brambles and elderberries – those weeds among trees.

Of the gates nothing was left but sodden fragments of wood. The posts also had rotted and fallen. My companion, who was a professional valuer of land, turned to me as he marked the roll of the 25-inch Ordnance Survey map in his hand, and said: "This isn't worth five shillings an acre."

He meant the annual rent; though I had an idea that he considered the land itself, which had a tithe on it of seven shillings an acre, was hardly worth buying even at that figure; for later on he advised strongly against the buying of the farm.

The other afternoon, when the field and I were seven years older, I looked around as I stood under the wood of pines and tall sycamore poles. I stood on the "scald" patch, where seven years ago the rabbit-diggings had been numerous and white.

Today there was sign of but one rabbit. In place of the short, thin grey grass, which had never been grazed in years, and was thin because it was starved, a fine sturdy layer of rye-glass and clover was spreading in emerald lines through the stubble. A regular plant, as they say; and the finest clover plants of all were on the "scald" patch.

Down below were the meadows, with the thistles and rushes nearly extinct; two cuttings a year and close grazing had brought back the wild white clover and improved the texture of the pasture.

How may tons of rotted mud and reeds from the grupps had we pulled out and carted uphill to the scald patch? We must have spread 60 tons to the acre. On that patch our finest corn had stood during the past summer.

Both field and meadows looked young, fresh and healthy. Beyond the riverside carr I saw the pale blue of the sea. The sun was sinking towards the west; not yet sunset, but the trees, when I turned round again, were outlined black against the golden burnish of the sun shining through the wood.

The air was mellow; it was marvellously clear; it was the air beloved of artists, the clear pure East Anglian air; and the colours of the trees in the carr beyond the meadows were the spirit of Cotman himself.

Cotman, the artist whose works sold in his life-time for a few pence, saw the truth and told the truth in paint; he had the pure vision of the clear and single-minded countryman.

And, standing there below the wood, my mind empty of material details, I felt myself identified, with startling clarity, with the pure colours of the earth, sea and sky. It was as though I had seen them for the first time.

Were those colours to be seen on that day of November seven years ago? The colours were there, no doubt, but the spirit was not free to enter into them. The vibrations of colour were not received by the mind.

The mind was not in tune with them. It was diminished by the weeds, the neglect, the desolation. On that day I was fearful, for I was about to enter into a laborious and, I was informed, a hopeless undertaking, which could end only in hurt to myself and those with me.

I did not see the colours; I saw only the poor grass, the weeds, the brambles, the sodden and broken bits of wood that had once been gates – part of England in ruin.

I saw the system by which the home market has been denied to British farmers, because it was more profitable for town-minded financiers to lend money to backward countries, and to import cheap corn and meat as virtual interest on the money that was lent to those backward countries.

I saw the system, which had nearly ruined the land and the countryman, which had neglected the great Empire, which denied and frustrated all attempts to make any kind of resurgent change for the better, this system which lived by slumps and depressions, by the fall of one currency and the rise of another, which enriched the cunning few and impoverished the majority, culminating in a war to preserve itself – a war which, alas, along would bring suffering, to the majority which did not know and which scarcely cared "why things were the way they were."

The valuer said: "If you buy this land it will be against my strongest advice." I said: "I believe that a revival will come very soon; the writing is on the wall."

He said: "It is not my business to be a prophet. I am dealing with things as they are today, not as they might be tomorrow."

I saw the dole-queues in the towns – the heroes of tomorrow's battlefields – the dead who were yet alive – and I made up my mind to carry through my original purpose; to enter on a hopeless task and thus perhaps qualify myself to speak with authentic tones when the time came.

That was in 1936. Since then, much has happened. Farmers have the home market. Prices are stable. Many farmers have paid off the mortgages on their land – the death engagements – only to mortgage the same lands again in order to pay the taxes which help to pay for the war machine.

Many are worse off than before, though outwardly this may not be apparent. The farm labourer, too, is really no better off. Neither farmer nor labourer feels any true security. Wages may be double, prices may be stable; but there is no real security. During the war we accept the situation; but after the war?

The colours of the trees down by the carr, and the blue of the sea and the shape of the pines on the hill-crest are beautiful, for a moment; but until Truth comes to be the real motive force of human life; the spirit of beauty can be seen only in rare glimpses.

The Black Death

June 1945

Lilias Rider Haggard

"There was no city, nor town, nor hamlet... in which this plague did not carry off the whole or the greater part of the inhabitants. This pestilence lasted for two years or more before England was freed from it. When, by God's mercy it ceased, there was such a scarcity of labourers that none could be had for agricultural purposes – women and even small children were to be seen with the plough" – Contemporary account of the Black Death.

In the chancel of our church there is a brass depicting the figure of Philip Bozard, Gentleman, and Margerie his wife. Philip had four sons beside him, Margerie five daughters. All but one had their arms folded, which shows that eight of the nine children died before their father was buried in 1490. When I was a child that brass stood to me as a sort of symbol. Early history was full of colour and romance, but it was a world outside actuality. Here I could see the family who lived at the "Hall," the boys and girls dressed in queer stiff robes on the exact pattern of their parents. Besides, had not my mother told me that when she was small she went to the Hall and played with the Bedingfeld children, whose ancestor was that very Philip upon the brass, in fact one of the boys was named after him. Thus the past was linked to the present in concrete form, and it has always seemed to me that it is true of the period in which Philip Bozard lived. It is in the fifteenth century that our village, rising from the ruin left by the Black Death, appears as a familiar scene with buildings and people whom we know.

The peasants and small farmers had won a stake in our village lands after the Conquest, and were rising towards independence, but it was not long before the land itself rebelled. The usual custom of cultivation was a three-year rotation: 1, wheat or rye; 2, barley, oats or beans; 3, fallow, when the cattle were turned in to graze but this was not enough. True, the fields got an occasional marling or liming, but manure was scarce. There was only just enough winter feed to maintain breeding animals and draught oxen, everything else was killed and salted down at Michaelmas. It was apparent that more and more land was needed to produce corn for bread, for the eight bushels of wheat an acre (which was the average yield) could not be maintained.

Actually in the year 1300 East Anglia was the richest place in England, paying the highest tax to the exchequer*, but this was largely caused by the prosperity brought to the villages by the Flemish weavers, and the expansion of the wool trade. Even so it was essential that all the population gave a hand with the land and it is believed that the Long Vacation from the Universities originated at this time, so that the growing numbers of young men sent to monastic and other colleges might help with essential field work in summer. For the owner of the "Manor House" began to realise that something was wrong, wages instead of feudal service upset the balance, the production of food was insufficient to support the estate and failed to tally with his labour bills and outgoings. In fact, the Manor had ceased to pay, even in good seasons. In bad years famine became acute, corn rising to five times its normal value. Then in 1348 it rained from Midsummer until Christmas, a sodden harvest lay on water-logged fields, and in August came the news of a terrible pestilence in Southern England brought by ships from the East. Next spring it appeared in Norfolk, and slew and slew "until well-nigh half mankind was slain," and there were none to bury the dead. They lay where they fell or were cast into open pits, afterwards called "No Man's Land," for none must touch the soil for fear of infection.

We do not know exactly what happened in our village, but there is a record of others like it in Norfolk. More than half the inhabitants were wiped out. The mills were silent because the millers were dead, the open fields covered with thorn and thistle, cots and crofts empty, the gardens and buildings round the deserted manor a ruin. The churches "were left to birds and beasts," the clergy, monks and nuns reduced to a handful, and the lands from which they drew their support largely derelict, for now befell the problem of labour. The scourge of the poor (for pestilence killed most amongst the ill-nourished and overcrowded) proved their opportunity. From all parts came the cry for workers. In vain did the King command no labourer should work off his Lord's estate or receive more wages than before, so "elated and contentious" were they that if any would hire them they must pay "their proud and covetous desires" or lose their harvests. The landowner was helpless, the labourer had become master of the situation, and started those "alliances and congregations" which were the parents of the Trades Unions. With recurring revolts and the pressures of economic problems on the landowners the Feudal System broke down, many serfs and villeins were free men, but they had lost their rights in the land, and created not a large class of peasants owning small plots, but a small class of large landowners paying wages for labour or letting land for rent. In fact, a social revolution had happened.

If we looked at our village of Ditchingham in the year 1400 we should see a great change. The huge strip fields would be gone, for they could not be used except by co-operative labour; the labourers were dead, and the new tenants erected the fences and hedges which give England her distinctive appearance to this day. Many of the cottages grouped round Manor House and church would have vanished and been rebuilt on outlying rented holdings. Men did not know that fleas and rats carried the plague, but they did know that burning their cots and building afresh someway off checked its ravages, and thus the village began to spread to scattered farms. The Lord of the Manor, unable to cultivate his demesne, said: "I will enclose it – sheep need less labour than crops – my land shall go down to grass." So we see the birth of "enclosure" and "parks", and also the increase in the already established wool trade which was to be called "the flower and strength, the revenue and blood of England." As the 15th century passed our village had evidently more or less recovered from the Black Death, for in 1479 they started to build a fine new church on the site of the old one, the Canons and monks from Norwich coming out to lay the foundation stone of the tower which stands in all its beauty to this day. Philip Bozard, of Ditchingham Hall, must have been almost the first to be buried in it eleven years later. His son and grandson lie in the nave, a very tall man and a little boy according to their brass, which prove to be true, as some 400 years later my father saw their skeletons.

*A sack of wool or its money value for every 610 acres. The usual tax was a sack for every 1570 acres.

My Estate

October 1946

Eric Fowler

The other day, being a ratepayer of Norwich, and therefore, as I conceive of it, a shareholder in the concern, I took a walk down Tuckswood Lane to see how the Corporation were getting on with the new housing estate that is being built in the neighbourhood. For all the depressing things that have been said about the slow rate of building and for all the rawness and mud of half-finished houses on a new site, I came away surprised by a sudden revelation of the immense social change that has taken place within my own lifetime – which is yet not a very long one.

Take bathrooms, for instance. All these little houses were being built with excellent bathrooms and hot water supplies. Thirty years ago bathrooms were comparatively new in the homes of many quite prosperous middle-class people in Norwich. People still lowered themselves uncomfortably once a week into hip-baths. On the other six days they washed in their bedrooms – and at this present time I find a belief lingering among some of the older generation that daily baths are liable to be bad for the health.

In winter they boasted of the film of ice on their water, for no bedroom had a fire in it except in case of sickness. As for manual workers, many were ingenious if ever they contrived to have a bath at all in their own homes, especially those that lived in the courts and yards of the city, in "one-up-and-one-down" houses. The one downstairs room was living room, dining room, kitchen and laundry for the entire family. The upstairs room was supposed to serve as a bedroom for all of them. Decency, not to speak of overcrowding, usually compelled some to sleep in the hard-worked downstair room.

There were often 20 such houses in one yard. The yards contained a standpipe which was the water supply for all the houses. They also contained a row of "privies", which served all the families in common and were often within 10ft of the living room windows. The narrow courts were perpetually hung with washing. They were dark. They smelt of humanity, greasy water and worse.

These houses were all that the builders of the time of the Industrial Revolution considered necessary for working-class families – and many families of 12 children were born and bred in them. Their playgrounds were the streets. The back-to-back houses of the northern towns and mining villages are worse, but the Norwich courts were bad enough. In them, mothers became old at 30. Some kept the dark little rooms pathetically clean and tidy. Some – small blame to them – became sluts. Men took to drink to get out of their squalid homes. Youths formed little gambling schools on the pavements, and scattered at the approach of a policeman. Girls spent their evenings perambulating the better-lit shopping streets, and not a few of them "got into trouble" in that way.

Respectable and responsible citizens blamed the slum-dwellers, but those respectable and responsible citizens didn't live in the yards and courts. The "one-up-and-one-downs" were well hidden from the public eye. If you didn't want to see them you needn't.

I was one of the respectable, and I was a snob. Most children are snobs. Some of them grow out of it. I would have walked a mile to avoid going through Ber Street, or King

Street, or Barrack Street.

I know now that King Street and Ber Street, at least, are fine streets, containing beautiful and historical buildings, and that the slums were an imposed ugliness, not inherent in those streets. But then they seemed to me to be just ugly, dirty places, inhabited by dirty, ugly people.

I didn't know why most of the men and nearly all of the children I saw there were ragged; why many of the women were toothless and shapeless; and why the little shops looked mean and flyblown. I judged by appearances and blamed the people.

There were some who never grew out of that attitude, and they were the highly respectable souls who in the 1930s objected to slum clearance and to council houses. The slum-dwellers, they said, would always be slum-dwellers. No doubt there are some bad tenants in the council houses built to replace the slums. Nine out of ten of them were the victims of their environment.

But the pre-war estates are excelled by the new ones. In these little brick or steel houses now being built, mainly for poor people, there is a standard of comfort not dreamed of even by the comparatively wealthy 30 years ago.

As I wandered around the half finished houses on the Tuckswood Estate and saw the way in which they were to be equipped, I could hardly believe it was less than 10 years since I saw some of the "one-up-and-one-downs" being demolished; not much longer since in one of the yards I talked to a mother who had lost four children in a year from one disease and another of poverty and overcrowding; and only thirty years since my father installed in our own comfortable house the great innovation of a bathroom and indoor sanitation.

You cannot yet call the council estates beautiful. But they certainly have the virtues of comfort and convenience. That will not of itself make us a more virtuous or a more high-minded people. But, by Heaven, there were some powerful impediments to virtue and high-mindedness in those old yards of Norwich, and – speaking as a very small shareholder – I am not displeased with my investment in the Tuckswood Estate.

Lilias Rider Haggard

November 1946

Eric Fowler

I am going to write an appreciation of a new book by Lilias Rider Haggard – "A Norfolk Notebook" (Faber, 8/6). I doubt whether I am the right person to do it, because my attitude towards anything she writes about Norfolk is uncritical.

It depends upon a personal and sentimental memory of a time in 1943, when I was stationed in what seemed to me a particularly unhappy part of India – scorched, arid and famine-stricken. It was then that I received as a present Lilias Rider Haggard's "Norfolk Life," and, reading it, was carried away in thought to my own country.

The cracked white earth of the rice fields, seeming to quiver in the sun's glare, and the thin patches of scrub, ill-nourished in the shallow soil over laterite rock, were clouded with the vision of the snug green valley of the Waveney on an autumn evening. The little, starved, straw-fed cattle of the Indian road were forgotten in a memory of fat red bullocks grazing on the marshes, their legs concealed, and their bodies seeming to swim, in a white sea of mist.

Nostalgia even conquered the smell of the Indian village, compounded of dung-fires, dust, urine and spices, and substituted the clean, cold, damp and bitter-sweet scent of the Waveney water-meadows. The plain no longer stretched flat to the horizon. The valley of my imagination rose softly into rich brown ploughland. The skyline was but a mile away, and was crowned with a thicket of oak and thorn, outlined against a sky whose billows of cloud were coloured black and gold by the sunset.

And for a little while I was healed of a helpless sorrow for the emaciated Bengalis whom I saw daily crouched beside the railway track, scrabbling amongst the ballast for any grains of rice that might have slipped out of a passing railway truck, and ever hoping to steal a ride to some place where there might be food for them.

Perhaps it was wrong to forget at any time their limbs like sticks, their sharp ribs and their piteous, high-pitched begging, but forget it I did for a while in a picture out of "Norfolk Life" of my own thick-shouldered, red-faced folk, with their slow, deep voices, their stubborn independence, and their quiet irony.

"Norfolk Life" was a reprint of extracts from the "Countrywoman's Diary" which Miss Rider Haggard had contributed to the "Eastern Daily Press" for many years, and "A Norfolk Notebook" is a continuation of those same extracts, covering the years 1938 and 1939. These books are something more than a diary and more than journalism, for they have a permanent literary value. There are few things so transient as literary reputations, yet I would consider it probable that Lilias Rider Haggard may be read a century and more hence – and that not merely because of her descriptions of ways of life that may then be forgotten, but because of her wholesome countrywoman's philosophy, and because of the beautiful and unforced prose in which she writes of things that centuries will not change. As I read "A Norfolk Notebook" I marked certain passages as eminently "quotable," but it is hardly necessary to do that with a book you can open at random and find things like this:

"It was one of those still evenings of autumn which seem to hold an illusion of spring. The pale rain-washed sky, the wet warm smell of earth, tentative scraps of song from birds beginning to recover from the silence of the moult, a partridge jugging on the plough, and a couple of big bats hawking under the shelter of the woods. Only the blueness of the shadows in the hollow, and their depth beneath the sharp tilt of the barn roof jutting up against the skyline, the bright gold of new corn stacks, and the purple blackberries and scarlet hips tell a different tale. The day faded out, slowly emptying the world of light, a cold, young moon sailed up over the common, and I called the dogs and went home contentedly to supper and a wood fire."

The unfinished sentence – a little catalogue of things seen, or rather felt as well as seen – is a favourite trick of hers, but not used so often as to become tiresome. It helps to keep up the modest pretence that these are just the jottings of a diarist; but how careful is the observation, how exact the choice of words! I thought I might have over-estimated "Norfolk Life" because of the mental and physical unease from which it gave me a temporary respite, but on reading "A Norfolk Notebook" in the (to me) luxurious cold of an English autumn, I realised that it was not so. I know of no writer who can distil into words so pure an essence of this well-loved county.

I caution the reader again, that even when I am at home Miss Rider Haggard suits my idiosyncrasies. The Waveney Valley is home for me, as it is for her. Next to that valley I love the flint villages, the creeks and the opalescent mud and sands of the North Norfolk coast and so does she. We even surrender in common to the comedy of ducks. Look at this:

"I borrowed a coloured drake from the farm to keep the ducks company until I can find an Aylesbury for them... The Ladies bowed and curtsied and bridled in the corner of the pond for all the world like a collection of simpering girls, while the gentleman sailed proudly in the middle, conversing at intervals in dignified quacks. Alas, by next morning he had decided he preferred wives brown instead of white and set forth on a pair of short orange legs on an adventurous journey across unknown fields back to the farm pond. Bertha, Belinda, Martha and Matilda, scorned and deserted, have abandoned coquetry and returned to mud dibbling in an inverted attitude, unromantic but satisfying."

With all this I have done no justice to the erudition, concealed rather than paraded, which illustrates the diary with apt quotations from anything from the classics to the Norse sages, digs out half-forgotten scraps of Norfolk folk lore, discourses of herbs and simples, touches on astronomy and, in a practical vein, is able to give hints on such technical subjects as the repair of clay-lump cottages. This is a wise book, and for all that it is overshadowed by war and the rumour of war, it is a happy book. It cannot be called "escapist," for some of the best passages treat of the war, but they treat of it in a proper spirit, which is neither of optimism nor of pessimism, but of faith. It seems that there are wise people who, in unhurried country occupations, catch a vision of eternity denied to us who live in towns, and "The Countrywoman" is one of them.

Gathering in the harvest at Methwold in 1951.

Harvesting in the early days of mechanisation.

Above: *Scottish fisherwomen gutting herring at Yarmouth's South Denes.*
Below: *Stacks of wheat and oats with their overhanging thatch at Diss in 1952. Note the flint bases to keep out rats and mice.*

Wildlife in the city

January 1947

Eric Fowler

One of the strangest and most beautiful sights in our city under the snow has been the flock of seagulls flying around the Market Place.

Flock is too tame a word for them. It is associated with domestic creatures like sheep.

Seagulls, though they come inland for food in hard weather, belong to the vast wilderness of the sea. Even while they play the scavenger they are fierce and aloof as savages.

I know of no noun of assembly for them, but on the analogy of a murmuration of starlings, I would suggest a keening of gulls. There is a bleakness about that sharp cry of theirs that speaks of black cliffs and desolate sands; of gales and spray, and a great space of grey and restless seas. Masefield knew what he was about when he added, "and seagulls crying" as a last touch of evocation to his Sea Fever.

As I listened to that keening – so foreign to our snug Market Place, which is more accustomed to the coo of a fat pigeon – I imagined the surge of the waves on an arctic coast.

In past years I have watched gulls by the hour from Cornish cliffs. I used to lie where I could look down on the stone roofs mottled with their droppings, and on the beach of the sunny cove, rowdy with their quarrel over the offal from the fishing boats.

Nearer home, I have seen the "kitties" whirl as thick as snowflakes over the herring dock at Lowestoft in autumn.

The shrill noise of their delight and greed mounts above the clatter of the drifters' winches.

I also remember watching gulls following the plough on a hill above the Stiffkey valley. They flew behind the ploughman like the white wake of a ship, and fluttered to earth for the worms exposed in the furrow.

I had a friend who wanted to photograph the gulls, but they rose at his approach and circled suspiciously.

"You want," said the ploughman, "to follow up an' down wi' me a time or two, to get them used to ye."

My friend followed up and down for half an hour in vain.

"Ah," said the ploughman, "that ain't no good s'arternune. They're got their bellies full, so they're right shy. You want to come fust thin o' the mornin, time they're sharp set."

So we left him, and scarcely had we turned our backs when the fluttering white wake reformed itself behind him.

But whether in the Cornish summer, the raw Lowestoft autumn or the cold spring of the uplands at Stiffkey, the sea was part of the picture, and the gulls were in it as a matter of right and beautiful commonplace. In the snow-clad city, they were utterly strange. The city itself is strange under a carpet of snow.

Its friendly and characteristic noises are muffled. It seems to change its shape as the whiteness of roofs and streets alters the pattern of light and shade. And if the frost be hard and the snow deep enough they interfere with the artifices we have come to accept as natural. Traffic is clogged, heating becomes inadequate, ice blocks the plumbing and we face all sorts of minor emergencies.

We have a sudden sense of the insecurity of civilisation. Nature is reasserting for a time her mastery over the arts of man. And as if to confirm this uneasiness, the sea birds shrill the call of the wild in the very Market Place.

I have felt no comparable emotion since a sweltering day in high summer, when I saw a group of gipsy women striding through one of our staid city streets. The swarthy gipsies seemed as much creatures of the sun as the seagulls now seem part of the frost and the snow – and they were as wild and strange.

Their colours were as garish as the colour of the gulls is pale, but just as inconsonant with the city. Their clothes were bedraggled, yet gorgeous with touches of scarlet, green and saffron. Their eyes were dark, bold and wary as the eyes of sea birds. One suckled an olive-skinned baby as she walked. I knew no more of these women's purpose than I know of the purpose of a seagull. Probably it was to sell clothes pegs or tell fortunes – as one might say the purpose of the gulls is to scavenge – yet there was something proud and secretive about them.

Ragged and harsh-featured as they were, the gipsy women had more grace and surety of movement than the sober and pallid citizens – even as the flight of a gull is more beautiful than that of a plump Guildhall pigeon. They looked finer animals.

The drab city people yielded them the full width of the pavement and eyed them with distrust. At that, the mother laughed high and suddenly.

I had the same feeling then as I have today about the sight and sound of the seagulls in the Market Place – that a sign had come into the city to remind it of the wilderness from which it sprang and to which it may eventually return. In the outer wilderness of the world life is lived but to survive and reproduce itself, and in achieving that, achieves beauty and strength but no law and no morality. There is something frightening about that kind of beauty. It is so scornful and indifferent to civilisation, even while it stoops to pick up its leavings – stoops, but never settles – and depends upon its eternal journey as mysteriously as it came, leaving nothing behind but the echo of a harsh, derisive cry.

Hornbutton Jack

February 1947

Eric Fowler

Searching a file of old newspaper cuttings the other day, I came across a series of articles written in Norwich in 1901 to celebrate the turn of the century. They were entitled "Norfolk in the 19th Century." There were eighteen serious and well informed articles touching on nearly every aspect of the life of the county, but the one that most tickled my errant fancy was that in which the writer had relaxed into an account of "Norfolk Oddities." If ever anybody comes to write in the year 2000 an account of "Norfolk in the 20th century," I doubt whether he will find such material for a tale of oddities as existed in the 19th century. We think of the 19th century as of the period which formed and strictly observed the staid conventions of the English middle class, yet when we look for brilliant or amusing eccentricities, we find such interesting freaks moving across the drab background of the Industrial Revolution, as we are at a loss to discover in our own time. In our day, to call a man "conventional" is almost to use a term of reproach, yet at this time when everybody likes to think of himself as unconventional, it is rare to find anybody who makes such significant breaches in the conventions as to become conspicuously eccentric.

However the rot – the relapse into a standardised mode of dressing, talking, behaving, living and even thinking – was beginning in the 19th century, and our journalist of 1901 betrayed it when he had to claim as his principal 19th century oddity a character who really belongs to the 18th century, inasmuch as he lives the first seventy years of his life in it, and only the last nine in the 19th century.

This was John Fransham – otherwise Hornbutton Jack – the son of the clerk of the parish of St. George, Colgate, in Norwich, who earns himself a place in the Dictionary of National Biography not only for his eccentricity, but for his scholarship. The foundation of his scholarship was laid by a well-to-do relative who paid for him to be educated by the Church – with the unexpected result that the classical learning he then acquired led him in later life to acquire a reputation as a pagan, writing hymns to the ancient gods, designating chicken broth as a sacrifice to Aesculapius, and describing a change in the weather as Juno's response to supplication.

However, the wealthy relation died when Fransham was 13. His father then objected to the cost of his education and upkeep – referring particularly to the cost of his shoes – whereat the youth went barefoot for the next three years. He was apprenticed to a cooper at Wymondham, but ran away, and earned a scanty subsistence by writing sermons for clergymen. He worked for an attorney, and later for a learned veterinary surgeon, who employed him to take horses to be shod, and taught him mathematics. When he was 18 he joined a band of strolling players. They got no pay and lived on turnips, and he left them on finding the turnips were stolen.

He then took ship at Yarmouth, designing to study at the Scottish Universities, but he disembarked at Newcastle and enlisted in the Old Buffs, who discharged him because he was bow-legged. He walked back to Norwich, and reached home with three-halfpence and a plaid he had bought on the way. He found work with a free-thinking weaver, with whom he carried on discussions above the rattle of the looms. About 1750, however, he found his vocation. He became a tutor, and a very successful one, for all his eccentricities.

He was described as short and thick-set, wearing his hair flowing over his shoulders. He dressed in a green jacket with large horn buttons (which gave him his nickname), a very broad hat, and large shoes. He wore his greatcoat indoors, and took it off when he went out. He lived from preference in a garret, where he would never allow the floor to be wetted or the walls whitewashed for fear of damp; yet he considered it "the height of effeminacy" to have his bed made more than once a week. The death of a pupil leaving him short of money, he tried to economise by sleeping on Mousehold Heath, wrapped in his plaid, but he caught a cold and gave it up. For a time he lived on a farthing a day. He bought daily a farthing's worth of potatoes, and each day he put aside one potato to pay for the salt.

When he had money for pleasure he judged it were better for some admixture of pain, so he would gorge himself with cakes and tarts until he had obtained a satisfactory ache – and then cured it with draughts of strong tea, to remind himself of the pleasures of health. He loved horses but hated dogs as "noisy, vulgar and mobbish," and in his "Aristopia, or ideal state" he provided for their extermination. He used to amuse himself by playing the drum and the hautboy, until one day he tired of the hautboy and used it to make a fire to brew himself some tea. He then acquired a passion for the game of "bilverketch," or cup and ball. He played it while he walked the streets and while he waited for pupils, and persevered until he could catch the ball on the spike 200 times in succession. He also kept count of the number of times he had caught it, and at the mystic number of 666,666 he gave it up.

He died in a garret in Elm Hill, and even as he had had his own manner of living this life, so he had his peculiar fashion of departing from it. He desired his nurse to lift him from his bed into his chair and, when he had ceased to move, to shake him well, and place him by a large fire with a hot apple pie under his nose. If these measures failed the nurse was finally to ask some beautiful woman to sit by his side – "For," said Hornbutton Jack, "if this last experiment do not succeed, then you may safely conclude that I am indeed dead."

I doubt whether the annals of the twentieth century will produce anything to equal that – but, as I think of Hornbutton Jack and his "bilverketch," I am reminded of the more recent craze for a toy of wood and string called a "yo-yo"; and it occurs to me that follies are now mass-produced and even our eccentricities have no individuality. He who writes of the oddities of the twentieth century will have to write about mass-movements and not about idiosyncracies.

Regimental Museum

June 1947

Clifford Butler

Next to gas lectures, when I did my early Army training, I disliked most the back-aching labour of anti-aircraft drill with the rifle and the wet-day tedium of talks on regimental history. Talks on the drab topic of military hygiene were much more diverting, chiefly because they were given by a medical officer who was an Irishman with an entertaining manner. I never expected to cultivate regimental pride, any more than I expected to have to deduce from their smells the identity of poisonous gases, or to shoot down an army aeroplane with a bullet. I expected, however, one day I might have to dig an Army swill pit, so the doctor was favoured with some of my attention.

Expectations are just as easily confounded as fulfilled in the unexpectedness of life. I had to dig many swill pits. I was right in my expectations about gases and enemy aircraft; I was lucky, perhaps. I was wrong when I expected I should never be proud of being a member of the Royal Norfolk Regiment; it took some years for the pride to develop, but it did so long before the end, and has intensified since. I disapprove of the principle of military conscription in peace-time, but since it has to be, apparently, I regret that the period of service is so short: it will give hardly anyone the chance of passing far enough beyond the buffets to come to like the life and it will give scarcely enough opportunity for the cultivation of regimental pride.

I must be fair, though, and admit that pride in a regiment is dependent on various things. More than anything else, it depends on having had to fight with it and on having had to share the pleasure and pain of active campaigning in company with men who comprise it, and whose memory will always be associated with its name. Real pride comes, however, when a sense of kinship is felt with the many thousands of men who served the regiment in the preceding two or three hundred years of its history.

I was never so much aware of such kinship until I went the other day to see something which proved vividly to me the reality of the almost imperishable continuity of my regiment. The red-brick Britannia Barracks, headquarters of the Royal Norfolk Regiment, stand more fairly than many other military headquarters on the Mousehold hills overlooking almost the whole of the city of Norwich. In the barrack yard is a large hut, which is regimental property inside War Office premises. It was built about 1900 for the use of the Militia, and bought by subscriptions from battalions in 1934 for conversion into a regimental museum. In the years since, its exhibits have been presented by various people rescued from the obscurity of officers' and sergeants' messes, and salvaged from refuse dumps. During the war, the museum fell inevitably into decline and disorder. Its recent renovation has been largely the work of Major R. D. Ambrose and his wife.

Major Ambrose joined up as a private soldier at Britannia Barracks in 1909, and is the present secretary of the Royal Norfolk Regimental Association. He showed me round the museum, and it was in the midst of the mementoes of the past that I sensed my kinship with the men who buried Sir John Moore at Corunna; fought and died of sickness in the squalor of the Crimea; were as much at home in the mountains of the North-West

Frontier as in the plains of South Africa; and in the 1914-18 war earned for their King's colours the honour of Mons, Le Cateau, Marne, Ypres, Somme, Hindenberg Line, landing at Suvla, Gaza, Shaiba and Kut Al Amara.

I felt a kinship with one man in particular. I never knew him, of course, but I served with his son who was a friend of mine. Private Charles Crampion won the Distinguished Conduct Medal for gallantry in Burma while serving with the 2nd Battalion in May, 1889; his son, another Charles, serving also as a private soldier with the same battalion was killed in Burma in May, 1944, within a few miles of where his father earned his decoration. The senior Charles' medals are in the museum, presented by a daughter. They include two D.C.Ms. and, for that reason, may be a very unique collection. Charles, senior, performed another gallant action in South Africa in 1900. He was sent another D.C.M. by the War Office. What should have been sent was a bar to the earlier award, and the War Office discovered its mistake later, but Charles, senior, kept his two medals.

It would take a lot of space and a long time to say something of all the interesting things in the regimental museum. Mementoes of the war just gone include the parchment recording the conferment on the regiment of the freedom of Norwich; photographs of the regiment's five V.Cs.; guns, swords and daggers captured from Nazis; and a piece of Japanese artillery. Among the older things are fragments of old Colours, which used to be the property of the various colonels and were cut up into pieces for their friends when new ones were presented. There are lots of medals and ancient uniforms and headgear; a water colour by a private soldier of the storming of the Khyber Pass in 1842; some Militia badges, including one awarded in 1800 for "military virtue"; a bell from H.M.S. Norfolk; an astonishing blunderbuss-cum-cannon taken in Tibet in 1904 and two Maxim machine-gun barrels worn smooth during that expedition. There is a suit of Saracen chain mail, a Crusades relic handed down as an heirloom from tribesman to tribesman, and worn by a Dervish in the Sudan in the 1890s.

There are many more things than I have mentioned. Within the walls of that hut in the yard of Britannia Barracks it is possible to re-create two and a-half centuries of military history. I saw enough to make me wish that I had listened a little more attentively to those wet-day talks. I should have had a little less to learn now.

This convenient car parking space by Orford Place was created not by the council but by Hitler's Luftwaffe.
Curls department store stood on this spot until April 1942 when it was destroyed during the infamous Baedeker Raids, the Germans' attempt to blitz Britain's cultural centres. The attack on the commercial centre of Norwich left 228 dead and 700 injured.
The site is now the home of Debenhams.

ICI
IMPERIAL

Carters
RTERS TESTED SEEDS LTD
INFORMATION
INFORMATION
SMITH & DERBY
CLOCKMAKER
SHEEP SHEARING
CATTLE
SHEEP
PIGS
HORSES
GOATS
PIGS
FORGE
OVERSEAS VISITORS PAVILION
PUBLIC CAFE
MEMBERS' DINING ROOMS
TRACTOR RING
Nº 1 ENTRANCE
DAY NURSERY
BANKS

The Royal Norfolk Show is about more than just livestock and agriculture. In this 1955 photograph, a couple of lads take a close look at an 18-pounder of the Royal Artillery.

Previous page: *The Royal Norfolk Show in 1957. The show was first held at the Costessey site in 1954, before which it had been peripatetic.*

The Royal Norfolk Show

June 1947

Eric Fowler

As far as I am concerned you can keep all your national and international exhibitions, if you will give me one agricultural show to enjoy. In general, I loathe the process of trooping round exhibitions and staring at exhibits. They are a crick in the neck, a headache, a soreness of the feet and a weariness of the flesh to me. Yet at an agricultural show I am happy.

The crowd of knowledgeable, sunburnt, farming people, who move leisurely about their holiday, never seems oppressive. The trampled grass is as sweet to walk on as to smell. You can always rest your eyes on trees when you are tired of looking at exhibits. And the exhibits themselves, the huge, muscular horses, the sleek and beautiful cattle, the curled and barbered sheep that look nearly as artificial as a barrister's wig, and the immense, shiny and somnolent pigs, all seem to me better worth inspection than a great deal of man's handiwork.

I suppose that point of view is an anachronism. So, to a certain extent, is an agricultural show. The high-stepping hackneys, that seem to dance round the ring, hardly belong to an age that has no more use for gigs and carriages but goes about in motor cars. The magnificent draught horses, which I regard as the emperors of the show, divide their kingdom with the tractors in the implement park. And how often in what I may call real life, as distinct from the pageantry of an agricultural show, do you see what I saw at Keswick Park on Wednesday – a team of four horses drawing a heavy wagon? To be precise, there were two such teams, and in my eyes at any rate they were the actors who stole the show. They were doing nothing which could be done nearly ten times as quickly and much more simply by a motor lorry, but no engine in the Motor Show ever has or ever will display its horse-power so magnificently as those two teams of glossy Suffolks, whose coats rivalled for brightness the twinkling brass of their harness.

I never saw a streamlined motor car with a finer curve than the lines of those lumbering wagons. An exhaust pipe never made music like the bells, the brasses, and the chains on the harness, or the creaking of the massive wheels. No machine ever expressed strength so eloquently as the walk of those horses. No cellulose panelling is more resplendent than a newly-painted farm wagon.

My neighbours at the ringside put the spectacle into words more tersely, and more eloquently, than a townsman can.

"D'ye like Suffolks?" asked one.

"Ah," said the other "They're clean-legged, ain't they?"

"Shouldn't wonder if they weighed a ton apiece."

"Ah, shouldn't wonder."

"Lovely, ain't it, to hear them old wheels a-bracken like they used to?"

"Lovely!"

Bracken is, of course, exactly the right word for the noise a wooden wheel makes when it turns on the axle of a heavy cart, but I wonder how much longer the word will survive. Only one of the wagons I saw on Wednesday had wheels that bracked. The other one ran on pneumatic tyres – to great practical advantage – and soon there will be no wheels left that can brack, and an excellent word will die away with the sound it imitated.

I shall long remember that centenary show at Keswick. It seemed to be the quintessence of all the agricultural shows I have ever seen and enjoyed. It had a perfect setting, with the tiny round-towered church and the surrounding trees for the background, and the grey hall, like an unobtrusive host, offering the hospitality of its lawn to the august gathering of vice-presidents, yet modestly concealing itself behind the grand stand.

The weather also was perfect, at any rate for show purposes. For some reason my memory retains the traces only of sunshine at these shows, and conveniently excludes the melancholy of dripping tents, wet feet, mired ways and umbrellas round the ring, on other occasions. It was perhaps best forgotten for the time being, that this particular sunshine was also the continuation of a drought that will make 1947 a black year in farming history – following, as it does, the worst winter of frost and flood in living memory. I believe even the farmers forgot it for a little while, enjoying while they could the success of their show. In its greenness and its air of carefree prosperity the whole thing did not seem quite real.

It contained so much of the old England mixed up with the new. It did not look as though there had been a world war, and before that an agricultural depression, and before that another world war, and before that another agricultural depression. It did not look as though the present was lean and hungry, the future anxious and the harvest likely to be scanty. On reflection, it seems to me to have been an illusion brought about by a green park, some hundreds of fine animals, a skilful organisation, and countrymen's determination to make the best of a holiday. On that day it was enough to be contented, like the sleek cattle, and take no thought for the morrow.

Selling family life

January 1948

Eric Fowler

Until lately I had never thought of sales by auction as melancholy or sentimental occasions. Then I attended a sale of the furniture of a relation of mine who has gone overseas to settle in the dominions. I had been brought up with many of the things that were sold, and it seemed like a betrayal of old friends that I should stand by and see them pass into the hands of strangers.

The furniture looked forlorn and shabby in the saleroom. The virtue imparted by affection had gone out of it. There were dust and scratches on the polished table that had once been a housewife's pride. Chairs and bedsteads, books and pictures, had become detached from their history and from one another. They were jumbled together with other people's furniture and had lost their identity.

They were like a family being sold in a slave market, where husband had been separated from wife, and children from parents, in the dealers' pens.

This, which the auctioneer called an occasional chair, had no longer any affinity with the sofa and those other chairs which still clung together as a suite. The suite was not a suite to us. Though they were alike in shape, pattern and colour, we knew each piece as an individual, just as parents distinguish the separate characters of identical twins.

The occasional chair, which did not match them in any particular, was part of them – bound into the family association by years of use, along with the carpet that now lay rolled up in a corner of the saleroom and the disgraced pictures standing with their faces to the wall.

We were unconscious of the blemishes on these things – or, at any rate, we were unconscious of them as defects. The smart young man from the furniture shop prodded the sofa and detected the broken spring. That would decrease its value for him, whereas for us it was a memorial of an incident in the childhood of Jack, who broke the spring when he was eight years old.

We Are Seven and AA Milne's other books for children were then so popular that they had also set a fashion for adults. Thousands of helpless babies were being christened Christopher Robin, and hundreds of boyish spinsters, who shared flats, were calling each other Pooh and Eeyore.

And Jack excused himself for breaking the sofa spring by saying he could not help being bouncy – which was a successful and, I believe, deliberate exploitation of the presence of the maiden aunt who had given him Winnie the Pooh.

The AA Milne books were roped together in a bundle for the sale, along with a large assortment of Penguins, the bound volumes of the Boy's Own Paper, dog-eared and torn by a large family of boys, and all the other books not considered valuable enough to be worth shipping freight. Various rough-looking dealers eyed them disparagingly, but would probably bid a few shillings for them.

Even the auctioneer's man was contemptuous when he packed them. He had highly specialised opinions on literature, for he confided that he hated books – not that he had ever read one, but they were difficult to tie up and kept slipping out of the bundle.

It was the miscellaneous lots, not even dignified with a mention in the catalogue, that caused me the greatest pang. The Primus stove, which the auctioneer's man produced out of a rusty tin hat box, with the air of a conjuror, was part of the equipment of the old Wave, and on Broads holidays I had fried sausages innumerable on it. I wondered what the purchaser would make of the hat box – there was a trick, that she would not know of, of using it to keep the wind from blowing the stove out.

I suppose it would have been useless for me to push my way through the crowd to tell her, and even more futile to tell the unshaven haggler who bought the engraving of Rosa Bonheur's The Horse Fair that that picture was valuable, because I lived with it for the first 10 years of my life, and knew every horse in it. I expect he bought it for the glass and the frame.

Ebb in the Yare

January 1948

Ted Ellis

January 8th
This afternoon I walked over to a little snipe marsh where the flowering bogbean sparkles and cotton-grass shakes out white billows of fluff in spring and where, through the summer broad, ribbons of various rushes and sedges weave a rich pattern in every shade of living green.

Today, in winter's fitful sunshine, the place looked desolate indeed – a brown and tousled waste, dark-pooled with flood waters, a sunken and dejected hinterland serving as a mere fore-stage foil to the shining reed beds beyond.

But when I waded into the bog (with care) and took a closer look at the vegetation, it became suddenly intricate and beautiful. The whorled branchlets of marsh horsetail were spread about like embroideries of silver hair. Flag leaves, grey speckled with moulds, lay in limp snaky tangles. The cotton grass formed soft red-brown tussocks through which could be seen their still living dark green leaf-bases.

Where last summer's rushes lay quite flat, new green spikes had grown through the mat like needles; and many a small green leaf was making the most of the winter daylight while taller competitors were laid low awhile.

January 10th
There is only a delicate lacing of snow on the fields here, forming rippled patterns caused by the interplay of sun and wind; but the ground is rock-hard, even along woodland glades, with sub-zero temperatures persisting day and night. Even so, moles are still breaking through the crust and I prodded soft earth newly pushed to the surface this afternoon.

Still pools are frozen firmly everywhere and now, swept by an icy blast from the east, even the tidal waters are fighting a losing battle with the frost, and wildfowl are to be seen congregating on rafts of ice where only yesterday they were swimming freely.

Except for the faint moaning of the wind and the cries of excited gulls here and there, a chill silence prevails, in the glare of winter's sunshine.

Looking across the marshes this afternoon, without a bird in view, I found most pleasure in watching the reed plumes, softly beating the air like wings of doves in their golden setting.

January 11th
With a new moon this morning we expected a spring tide; instead a southerly gale held back the oncoming flood in the North Sea, and as a result we experienced a continuous ebb in the Yare waters for 12 hours on end. Mudflats became exposed in the Broads round about midday, and by 8pm the water had reached the lowest level we have ever known here.

Rockland Broad came to look like Breydon, with high shelf-like mud banks intersected by branching channels.

In places water-lilies sprouting from the mud appeared to be growing on dry land and reeds round the shores stood in towering clumps, with three feet of stalk exposed below the usual cutting level, and with encrustations of sponges patching their blackened slimy bases.

Empty valves of freshwater mussels littered the mud, and as the white shell beds emerged in the Fen Channel, air got into thousands of little shells, causing them to float away.

We took the punt down as far as Rockland Fleet during the evening and found navigation quite a tricky business, what with shoals, jagged remains of water-borne trees and sunken wrecks.

For a time we lay under the shelter of the hulk of a sunken wherry, her stern, complete with rudder, high and dry; the old boat seemed to have come to life again after having lain hidden under a thick blanket of mud, reeds and sallow bushes for many years.

The birds we noticed seemed slightly awed and nervous – acutely aware of a strangeness in their surroundings. In the lantern light a moorhen fluttered as light as a moth and dropped straight into my lap in the boat, while a huge coypu skulked stolidly on the shore, eyeing us with interest.

The food of love

February 1948

Eric Fowler

Listening to music is, for me, the highest of all pleasures. Yet I make little use of a wireless set or a gramophone. Gramophone music is constantly interrupted by the necessity to change the record. The cranking, and the turning of records, interrupts the musical mood.

Wireless sets are even more exasperating. I have never yet encountered a set so perfect that it did not on occasions develop horrible noises called atmospherics, or cause the sound to fade, or accompany symphonies with an obligato of jazz band and somebody making a speech in German.

The occasions on which wireless sets do this are always the important ones. They reproduce to perfection the inanities of dance bands or the football results, but whenever there is a concert to which I particularly want to listen, there is a mechanical interruption.

I am driven – willingly – to the concert hall. And quite apart from the mechanical imperfections of gramophones and wireless sets, there is surely some virtue in being present at a concert, hearing the living performers without the interposition of a machine, and being assisted by the concentration of hundreds or thousands of other people, who are also intent upon the music. The experience of listening gains intensity through being shared with many others. The common enjoyment magnifies that of the individual.

I go to concerts to enjoy myself, and generally I succeed. I am not one of those people who like to hold a post-mortem on every concert they attend. They dissect the orchestra and discover emaciation in the tone of the second violins and flatulence in the trombones. They take a sort of musical tape measure to singers and find sopranos lacking in altitude and basses in rotundity.

They weigh the chorus, section against section, and make the balance uneven. With the conductor they become psychologists, and accuse him of exalting his ego at the expense of the composers. Then they tear the programme to pieces, and declare either that it lacked novelty, or that it was monotonous, or that the various items were incompatible.

I sometimes wonder why they go to concerts at all. It seems to make them so unhappy. The answer, obviously, is that they enjoy being critical. If ever they go to heaven, they will not taste delight until they can discover an angel with an ill-tuned harp and complain about it to the Almighty.

On the other hand I cannot yield myself entirely to the enthusiasm of the promenaders, who do not feel they have done justice to any performance until they have clapped, stamped and cheered their approval for five minutes on end, with little or no discrimination between great music and that which is merely competent and entertaining. But I can understand why they do it. There is a state of exaltation induced by hearing fine music that demands some physical expression.

I was once impelled, out of sheer light-heartedness, to go from a concert at which Sir Thomas Beecham had conducted Mozart and Delius, to a dance, where I mixed my drinks and made love in extravagant terms to a dull woman who lived at Surbiton and liked Henry Hall and ice hockey matches. It took all that to bring me down to earth again.

A musician, I suppose, can discharge these emotions by making music. Having had the Philistine upbringing which was usual for British youth 20 years ago, I am incapable of doing that. I was dismissed at the age of 10 from our weekly "music class", which consisted of singing the better-known English ballads in unison, with a thumping lead from the piano. I was said to be a premature bass – and flat at that.

I once knew a man who yearned to participate. He discovered, eventually, a piece in which the triangle had to be struck – once. He importuned the conductor of an orchestra until he was allowed to put on evening dress and sit as a member of the orchestra, next to the drummer, with the triangle in his hand and a piece of music in front of him.

He had been carefully rehearsed in his part, but he was so lost in the enjoyment of his glory that when the precise moment came for the triangle to be struck, he miscounted the beat and the drummer had to strike it for him.

He used to weep when he told the story. Nowadays, I believe, they have classes in musical appreciation, choirs, and even orchestras, in the elementary schools, but the reform has come, alas, too late for the triangle-player, or for me.

Natural inspiration

December 1948

Lilias Rider Haggard

Sunday, December 11th

A grey day which later turned to gloom and rain. The darkest month of the year is with us: hardly anything stirs in the garden and one's business there is concerned almost entirely with roots.

In each lies a secret, the whole enchantment of spring, the burning heart of summer, the fruitfulness of autumn, locked beneath the earth in a network of finest fibre, odd-shaped tubers, and stout unromantic-looking bulbs.

There colour and scent are made, the greatest forest tree is conceived, the most fragile flower hid until "that great marvel outwardly appeareth, some milk white as the lily, some purple coloured as the violet and saffron flower, some scarlet red as the aramanth, some speckled as the carnation, some like that sad blue coloured flower as is calcedonie, so that man may see how nature worketh in many and hath abundantly bestowed her labour."

It is small wonder that our forefathers had such faith in roots, from the magic mandrake – which was supposed to cry in agony when dragged from the ground – to the plantain, "of all plants the most humble and the most virtuous."

Many of the wonders of the world were hid from them, but they had an infinitely greater appreciation of those that lay at their door. Roots were to them an essence of the plant itself – its virtue and comfort in concrete form.

As an old herbalist said, "This knowledge lays open to the wayfaring man – it grows in every field – it meets us in all our paths and was mercifully given to eradicate the pestilential seeds of infection."

Many that they used habitually are still the chief drugs employed in medicine, only this generation has lost nearly all knowledge of the use of plants and prefers them in a nice bottle from the chemist, coloured a delicate pink, and labelled "The mixture as before."

Monday, 12th

Very lovely in the early morning, with a veil of mist lying low over river and common, which the sun – rising behind a mountainous cloud bank lying with glowing peaks and dark valleys across the horizon – flushed to every shade of pink and saffron. Each twig was beaded with a dew drop, and the grass washed with silver, so that the moorhens chasing each other backwards and forwards with jerking tails and spasmodic cluckings in a sudden access of spirits, left little dark trails behind them.

From the wood came a chorus of song heard for the first time on the mild mornings of the last week, a chorus which will fall completely silent in frost and snow and bitter east wind, only to break out again every warm day until it swells to its full glory in spring.

It is led, as always, by the clear articulated loveliness of the thrush's notes, which for all their impassioned joyousness hold an equally impassioned regret in the reiterated

"Why-Why-Why-Why?" which made old William Allingham, striving to write down the thrush's song on paper, explain:

O thrush be still -
Or at thy will
Seek some less sad interpreter than I!

Tuesday, 13th

B brought down to me a slab of oak which he is going to make into a stool. He had taken it out of the river bank by the old mill-race. There has been a mill on this spot for centuries, but the earliest mention I have found is in the Parliament rolls as follows:

"William de Pirnhow in the 24th of Henry III, released to Roger Earl of Norfolk his right of fishery from the Mill of Cliff to the bridge of Bungay and the Earl granted him a fishery from Bungay bridge to the Earl's vineyard".

This would have been about the year 1250, and the mill was destroyed by fire about 1780 and never rebuilt. The plank formed the bed-plate of the mill wheel, and must have been under water for hundreds of years. There was some erosion of the wood on the surface, but when planed off it proved to be perfectly sound, completely blank oak, as hard as iron.

Thursday, 15th

There is no sign of Christmas in wood, field, or pasture, the grass is as green as April and the first flake of snow has yet to fall, but the shops are full of holly and the first of the mistletoe from abroad. My two bunches in the apple tree are thickly set with milky berries.

Not many people know that the tradition of kissing under the mistletoe comes down from before the dawn of Christianity, when it was used in pagan marriage rites. All parasites, even orchids, have their repulsive side. Plants are abnormal which refuse to touch mother earth unless she be transformed by some host, but the fleshy leaves of the mistletoe and its moonshine berries are the more so because it often seems to prefer a tree which is sick.

It was, however, always considered a fount of all virtues, averted evil from the hearth; a decoction rendered barren animals fruitful and deadly poisons harmless. But it must be cut with a golden knife and caught in a white towel so that it never touches the earth from which it shrinks.

It also demanded sacrifice – the blood of a white bull, whose horns had never been bound by man.

The house he use

November 1949

Eric Fowler

If you want to see Billy Smith, go you to the Goat and Compasses. That's the house he use.

People use public houses in Norfolk; they do not merely go to them or drink in them. There is a long-established custom in the word "use". Billy Smith is not one of your restless pub-crawlers, flitting from bar to bar. Neither is he one of your casual, occasional drinkers. You may depend upon it that at a certain hour every morning or evening he is to be found in the Goat and Compasses and no other house, that he has his own place and his own little circle of intimates – probably in the bar parlour or the smoke room – and that there he drinks a certain quantity of liquor each day as an accompaniment to sociable discourse. It is unlikely that he is a heavy drinker. He is merely a regular one. It is also probable that he drinks beer, not spirits. He may have a fancy to drink it out of pewter, and have his own particular tankard hung on a hook behind the bar, and reserved for him by the landlord. Only on high days and holidays will he get in the least elevated with liquor. He drinks beer because he likes beer, and because it is a sociable habit. But he turns a cold shoulder to drunkards. There is a stage at which they become a nuisance, offensive to the sodality of Billy Smiths in houses like the Goat and Compasses.

For the use of the Goat and Compasses is that of a club, and the house sets its own standard of decorum – lower, perhaps, than that of the Athenaeum, but none the less cherished. Honest oaths for the sake of emphasis are not discouraged, but habitual obscenity of talk is frowned upon. Broad stories are told, but indecency earns no laughter for its own sake; there must be seasoning of wit to set the bar parlour in a roar. In general, the talk is sedate and even philosophical. Some of it is shop, and a good deal of it is gossip about local events and people. The most impassioned arguments are about sport. Politics are often the subject of irony, but seldom of serious discussion, and the same applies to women. Encroachments upon the other really dangerous debating ground of religion are very rare, although somebody does occasionally wax critical of parsons.

There are no rules in this club, save the licensing laws; no entrance fees, save the price of a drink; and no powers to blackball or expel members, save for gross disorder. It is an extremely tolerant society, but it has its taboos and its own mysterious methods of enforcing them. Nothing overtly hostile is said or done to any frequenter of the Goat and Compasses who is uncongenial to Billy Smith and his intimates. Silently they study him and find him wanting, subtly they avoid drinking with him, and monosyllabically they block his conversational openings, until the Goat and Compasses' beer becomes gall and wormwood to him and he disappears to find his proper social level in some other house.

As for the Goat and Compasses itself – it is usually a small house; as likely as not with no amenities save a dart board. There has been much talk in recent years of reforming public houses – of making them large, light, airy places with restaurants and pleasure gardens, where a man can take his family, and the sale of beer and spirits is not the sole purpose of the landlord. The new public houses are mock-Tudor mansions, with their exteriors floodlit.

They have long bar counters glittering with chromium plate and decorated with sandwiches in glass mausoleums. There are big lounges full with tubular steel furniture with imitation leather cushions, shining under neon lights. They are crowded with as many women as men, sipping the same beer as is in the Goat and Compasses – yet somehow it is not the same.

Conservatives like Billy Smith and myself cannot get used to such places. They are too slick, spacious – and feminine. The Goat and Compasses, like most of the best clubs, is old-fashioned, snug and masculine. Women do enter it, but they can hardly be said to use it. They are there on sufferance, and they do not trespass within the inner circle of Billy Smith and his intimates. They converse among themselves, while their husbands and escorts are engaged in discussions of more moment. The Goat and Compasses does not accommodate them easily on its benches and hard wooden chairs, and they leave early. The place is full of friendship and comfort, but the friendship is of that unexacting and inarticulate kind that few women understand, and the comfort is only apprehensible by masculine senses. The reformed public houses may be a good thing. Billy Smith would no doubt regard it as preferable to prohibition – but not to the Goat and Compasses.

The City Debonair

June 1951

Eric Fowler

I write this on the morning after the Royal opening of the Norwich Festival, and I am still a little drunk with pride and pleasure. For good or for ill, the intoxication started on Sunday with that stately service at the Cathedral. I never see the west doors open, and the civic procession passing down the tremendous vista of the nave – the sword and mace bearers preceding the Lord Mayor in his black and gold, while the organ peals, and the choir sings the processional hymn – without an immense pride that I live on so stately a city. Thus, I reflect, does Norwich rise to a great occasion. Whether pride is the proper sentiment I do not know. The purpose on Sunday was humbly to dedicate the Festival to God, remembering the mercies vouchsafe to our forefathers, whereby they achieved greatness, and praying that we might show ourselves worthy of the city and the nation that they, for all their sins and errors, were inspired to build. The lesson, to rebuke our materialism and remind us of our spiritual weakness, was the Sermon on the Mount. "Blessed are the meek." Hardly I strove with the old Adam in me, being reminded by Satan of the saying of that gentle tempter, Robert Lynd, that he preferred it in the French version – "Blessed are the debonair."

And on Monday morning – alas for the promptings of the preacher – it was the debonair that triumphed over the spirit of humility. The crowds like a living border round the coloured stalls of the Market Place; the flowers and flags; the long scarlet banners pendent from the City Hall; the trumpeters in gold livery sounding their fanfare; the little white Princesses walking up the steps and speaking royally from the balcony; the noise of St. Peter's bells clashing and rollicking over the city; the aeroplanes shooting like a flight of silver arrows across the sky; the great sleek cars rolling smoothly past the Guildhall on a triumphal journey; the polite jostling and the inarticulate cries of these quiet people of ours, who are always too shy to cheer – debonair was the only word for it all. Norwich has never looked more fair than for this Festival, and was never more true to herself than when she declared flags of secondary importance and decked herself with flowers.

I went round the exhibitions. The Castle is magnificent. Crome's great dark painting of the windmill, with the white light behind it , shows in its new setting like a survival of the spirit of those dour, independent Flemings, great artists and fine craftsmen, whose stock was mingled with ours in Norwich nearly four centuries ago, and can yet be traced today in the patient, careful workmanship of our people, our specially independent protestantism, the round gable-ends in our old streets, and our many gardens. There is such a grand aggregation in the Castle now of the work of Crome, Cotman and their followers as will suffice for years of pleasurable study – yet I must turn aside and look also at that room which is hung with the etchings of Rembrandt. There is something peculiarly appropriate in the bequest of that collection to Norwich – and in its bequest at the very time when the city took into its custody the supreme collection of the Norwich School. Rembrandt is our kinsman; part of the parent stock of the East Anglian

The Norwich Festival procession in 1951, part of the Festival of Britain. Snap the Dragon is ushered through the crowds by the Whifflers and ***(below)*** *Queen Boadicea represents Norfolk through the ages.*

breed of Englishman.

Look next in Blackfriars Hall, which was once the Dutch church and see how obstinately survives in the Machine Age the delicate and meticulous skill of the craftsman, which was learnt and is inherited from Flemish weavers. Down the centre of the hall is a working range of the machines with whose aid shoes are made. But machines here are only an aid to the craftsman; they have not replaced him. For proof of that, look at the show cases of shoes ranged round the walls – shoes for children, for elegant walkers, and for dancers; shoes which, however great a part machines have played in their making, have been touched with art by the fingers of craftsmen.

Next, in the Evening, to the Odeon, to hear Sir Thomas Beecham conduct the opening concert by the Royal Philharmonic Orchestra. The conversion, for the nonce, of a cinema into a concert hall is a device which does equal honour to the public spirit of Mr Arthur Rank and the ingenuity of Norwich. Beecham made a royal occasion of it. He looks, in these days, uncommonly like the photographs of King Edward VII – although it is almost as difficult to imagine King Edward conducting an orchestra as to conceive of Sir Thomas Beecham becoming known to posterity as the Peacemaker. His music, as of old, is by turns delicate and fiery, and the sound of the trombones rings at his command like deep-toned bells. At the end, Tchaikovsky's flamboyant Fourth Symphony acted on the conjoined emotions of 2000 people as a more powerful cathartic than the spectacle on the streets. We filled the hall with wave upon wave of applause. We hoped, perhaps, to tempt the magician into speech – something of the hot-blooded kind for which he is notorious. But he, grave, elderly, and debonair, was content for his music to say all. Three times he retired, and was persuaded to advance again, but kept silent.

We went out into the moonlight, and I, by happy chance, walked back by old St. George's, and so encountered a fresh miracle. I stopped on the bridge, and there, above the roofs of Elm Hill and the trees of St. Martin-at-Palace, was the Cathedral spire, floodlit, and across the dark water lay that white pinnacle of stone again, reflected in every detail.

That sort of thing is supposed to happen only in Venice, or in Bruges. I went into the Festival Club at the Assembly House and talked extravagantly, slapped the august Festival Director on the back and told him he had made me very happy, and went out again to Chapel Field Gardens to dance under the coloured lights among the soldiers of the Royal Norfolk Regiment and their girls.

Whatever else happens in the Festival, Norwich has already had her hour and I have had mine. I shall be deeply ashamed of this article in print, for it comes perilously near to cheering, which in an East Anglian is a sin unpardonable.

Residents of London Street in King's Lynn are left stranded as the flood waters of January 31, 1953 surge through the town. ***Right:*** *the Queen, with the Duke of Edinburgh, visits Gaywood rest centre at King's Lynn, where thirty children evacuated from their homes sang nursery rhymes for Her Majesty.*
Overpage: *Swirling seawater pours through the gap at Sea Palling, demolishing everything in its path, during the 1953 flood.*

The sea's triple assault

February 1953

Eric Fowler

In times of gale and flood we become conscious in Norfolk we live on a promontory. It is, moreover, a promontory of chalk, grave, clay and loam, vulnerable on all three sides. Eastward, the sea scours away the beaches, breaks over the sand-hills, and tries to make again the great bay into which the rivers once emptied themselves separately, instead of being constricted as now into a single channel at Yarmouth. It was, as one may conceive, a shallow bay of sand and mud, interlaced at low tide with innumerable creeks and some broad channels. It would have been fringed with marsh and dotted with low islands which are now the villages of the Fleggs. To seaward there were sandbanks, one of which is now Yarmouth. Perhaps a freak of the sea, piling up sandbanks against itself, assisted the ingenuity of man – forever digging, draining and embanking – to produce East Norfolk as we know it, with its pattern of Broads and slow, muddy rivers, and the fresh-water marshes and ploughland in-between.

It looks a solid and settled pattern, but it is solid and settled only because man wills it to be so. The sea wills it to be fluid. Time and again – and never more dangerously than this last weekend – a gale helps to muster an immense tide with a furious sea atop of it, which attempts to restore the bay behind the protective arm of sand and clay that extends southwards to Happisburgh, with the South Denes at Yarmouth for its forefinger. It is a protective arm, but it is weak at the joints, where it has to be reinforced with concrete walls, groynes and revetments, as at Eccles, Caister and Yarmouth itself. Yet the sea still finds weak places. Moreover, the great tides run upstream and swell the rivers, which then conspire with the sea by pressing against landward embankments like the Breydon wall, by whose failure Cobholm is now flooded.

North-eastward from Happisburgh, soft, sandy cliffs rise towards the clay and gravel escarpments of Mundesley, Cromer and Sheringham, and here indeed the promontory of Norfolk looks strong enough, but the sea, although it cannot break in, nibbles away at the soft foot of the cliffs until they fall away, hundreds of tons at a time. Gales and tides like those at the weekend send it leaping in to smash seaside promenades, scour away the beaches and bite great chunks out of the cliffs wherever it finds them unprotected.

In the north, from Salthouse to Holme, the uplands recede, and there is a narrow coastal plain with a broad fringe of salt marsh, mud flats and sands, where the sea plays at will, until it strikes shingle ridges, or the earthen walls built to confine the creeks, protect the marsh, and defend the towns and villages at the mouths of the little rivers. Sand dunes planted with pines defend the great reclamations of the Earls of Leicester and Holkham. The villages are mostly on the higher ground, but wherever there is a little estuary, building has crept down to the marsh level to form what were once seaports and are now fishing, yachting and holiday villages. With the great gale and tide, the sea swept all over the marsh, and the creeks became broad rivers running inland. So it was that Salthouse was smashed, and Cley so cruelly devastated that dwellers inland may wonder whether the lower parts of either village will be populated again.

Westward, looking across The Wash, the chalk cliffs of Hunstanton form the hardest part of the Norfolk promontory – the end, as it were, of a backbone of chalk that extends southward under Breckland to the downs of Newmarket. But the intermission is very brief, and from Hunstanton southwards the coastal plain extends itself, and has been extended further by reclamation, towards the mud flats, sands and sea. Here again the sea has shown its power to return, and has most cruelly avenged itself on the bungalow settlements built, in the confidence of summer days, perilously near the sea level.

But even Kings Lynn, old as it is – and Yarmouth too for that matter – represent an adventure of man in establishing himself for the purpose of trade, as close to the sea as possible, and then century by century extending his settlement and making his footing more secure. There also the sea, maybe once or twice in a century, at the utmost reach of a great and savage assault, reminds him of the insecurity of his tenure.

And south of Lynn, along the western flank of the promontory of Norfolk, lie the Fens. It is hard for a stranger walking or driving across that flat and fertile expanse to realise that Ely, Queen of the Fens, and all her satellites were once islands, and that the rivers and dykes run above the fields. All this is land wrung from the water. And the land, since its reclamation, has shrunk like a dying sponge, so that the embankments have to be made ever higher and wider, the pumping and draining more elaborate. Fifty miles and more inland from Lynn, the safety of the land still depends on the sea level. The fall of the rivers is a matter of inches to the mile, and gale and tide can hold up the water in the mouth of the Ouse, so that it bursts the banks far inland and floods the farmlands.

The water spilling out of the Ouse and Denver, and spreading over the eastern Fens, is part of the same catastrophe and arises from the same cause as the salt tide running through the beach in the sand dunes at Palling, or the flood lapping over the wall of Breydon Water into the back streets of Yarmouth. We have been hit in Norfolk on three sides at once. The very spread of our civilisation – the housing estate at South Lynn, the land reclamation along the shores of the Wash, the bungalow population lining the cliffs and sand dunes – has increased our susceptibility to the blow. Years ago, perhaps it would not have mattered so much if a river had overflowed here or marshes been flooded there. Nowadays it all matters intensely, and we are left wondering what we can do, short of lining the whole coast with concrete. But there has been no time in our history when we are not fighting the sea, even as we used it for our commerce, and if today we are more vulnerable, we have greater engineering resources with which to defend ourselves.

Our Decorations

May 1953

Eric Fowler

I have been walking as far as one may in the morning, to see how Norwich is decorating itself for the Coronation. St. Giles', St. Stephen's, King Street, the Riverside, Prince of Wales Road, Magdalen Street, and St. Benedict's made a good walk on a fine summer morning, and the city looked beautiful – as indeed it always does when you clear your eyes of the scales of custom and habit, and see Norwich, as a stranger sees it, in perspective.

The customary view is the short view, that does not look much higher or farther than the shop windows and lower storeys of houses. It takes a novelty, like these street decorations, to make you look upwards and onwards. How often, for instance, do the native and the resident look over to the middle of the city from the far end of King Street, and see the Castle, St. Peter Mancroft, and the City Hall outlined above a great sweep of warm red roofs, embowered in trees, and studded with other towers?

The eye is attracted to that view now, because Carrow Works has embellished the far end, which is usually the dull end of King Street, with a fantasia of flags, banners, plaques, and spinning discs of coloured board, all strung up on lofty frames of tubular scaffolding and wire on either side of the street. It is eccentric and very gay, and you look beyond it to see into what sort of pleasure garden this fantastic avenue leads – and with the oddest of contrasts you see the city of towers and gardens; centuries old, serene and warm and industrious in the summer sunshine.

No other Norwich decorator, yet, has contrived anything so light-hearted as the airy decorations of King Street – and nothing so gay has come out of Carrow since those pleasantly crazy advertisements of the Mustard Club twenty-odd years back. Elsewhere draper's shops and general stores have become pavilions with banners, Royal portraits, and loyal emblems, and streets are all a-flutter with Union Jacks, but the bunting is disposed after a more conventional fashion, and there are no mad, surprising toys whirling among it.

Perhaps it was churlish of me, but as I walked I became a little dissatisfied with flags and banners. There is nothing we can do in this direction that Oxford Street and Selfridge's cannot do better – except those superb crimson banners that will in due course descend, as on other State occasions, from the parapet to the balcony of the City Hall. They, like the coloured canvas tilts of the market stalls, were an inspired decoration, and they have become an essential part of our local pomp and circumstance.

What we can do magnificently, as we discovered in the Festival of 1951, is flowers. How fortunate that as well as all our public gardens, and the window boxes we are learning to love, we can contrive garden beds in the streets to receive them! The window boxes are being prepared, and the garden beds are ready for the new stock of plants, but for the full glory of the flowers we have to wait a few days longer. It will be all right on the day, and with flowers to reinforce and outlast our bunting we shall salute the Queen the whole summer through.

It is flowers that are best in scale and keeping with Norwich. But they can hardly magnify the beauty that is already there in a city which is not so much grandiloquent as intimate, inspiring affection rather than astonishment. With its buildings new painted and its gardens specially trim for the Coronation, and the trees in their early summer verdure, Norwich is already beautiful, and it only needs now that the streets and squares shall be garnished with flowers.

I am not sure that Trory Street was not the most touching sight I saw – and Trory Street has no special graces. It is a humble little street of grey brick terrace houses on one side and red brick on the other. I chanced to see it because it is, so to speak, in my parish, and of a sudden it has been adorned with a triumphal arch of red, white and blue, and bridged from side to side with strings of flags.

How, I asked, had this happened? It then transpired that the people of Trory Street and its three neighbour streets had subscribed £90 for their own Coronation carnival and children's treat. Trory Street, as a cul-de-sac, had been chosen as the scene of the carnival, and "the boys" – which is to say the men of the neighbourhood – had put up the decorations at the weekend. They were not yet complete, for the triumphal arch, and the trees at the end of the street were to be illuminated.

Another of "the boys" was making a stage in his backyard, for an addition to the carnival and tea party there was to be a concert in the street.

"It's wonderful, the neighbourliness in this district," I was told, and so it is, and no doubt there is many another street or group of streets working in the same fashion, and astonished at its own unity.

That, after all, is the best of reasons why every town, village, or even street should have its own particular celebration of the Coronation, as part of the national celebration. It gives us a fresh consciousness both of our individuality and of our unity and loyalty to one another, which is expressed in loyalty to the Throne.

The Cattle Market

Autumn 1953

Eric Fowler

I took the children round the Cattle Market on Saturday. They are probably in the last generations of Norwich children to enjoy that treat. A friend of ours, a forcefully humane lady, greeted us as we were wandering about. "Are you watching the cruelty on the market?" she asked, pleasantly.

I was sensible that she was rebuking not only my presence but my thoughts, for I had been thinking it a pity that the market was to be moved out of the middle of the city. I suppose that was the wrong kind of sentiment, but the moving scene of Norwich Hill on a Saturday was part of my childhood. There was no room to park cars there in those days. The whole of the space between the Shirehall and the Agricultural Hall was full of sheep.

Beyond them were the fat cattle, with butchers and farmers in earnest colloquy about them, while out of the sale ring, through the lowing, the shouting, the sliding of hoof and hobnails and the clatter of sticks, you could hear the harsh monotone of the auctioneer.

And then, all the way up the steep slope of Cattle Market Street there were pigs – pigs ambulant, pigs somnolent, pigs in strident indignation being unloaded from carts into pens. At the top of the hill the pig pens merged into a nondescript market of poultry, rabbits, pigeons, ferrets, old bicycles and goats. But all this, crowded and clamorous as it was, made but the fringe of the Cattle Market.

From the pig pens clear across the wide open space and the avenues of plane trees to the wall beneath the castle stretched the store cattle – the rough red beasts shipped from Ireland and Canada to be fattened into prime beef on the Norfolk marshes and in the bullock yards.

Memory makes this scene autumnal, with a damp, bitter scent from the falling leaves of the planes, mixed with the all-pervading smell of kine, and the reek of the drivers' shag, and whiffs of their beer. There was a mist above the backs of our cattle. A fine drizzle bedewed their rough coats and the young steers milled about under the sticks of ragged Irish drovers, while Norfolk farmers in buskins eyed them with stolid appraisal.

It was a wild, noisy, bewildering and exciting spectacle to a little boy such as I was.

You were always in danger of being knocked over by runaway cattle, yelled at by drovers, or run down by carts, until you got into the comparative quiet of Bell Avenue, where to be sure there was still noise enough from the ceaseless talk of the stallholders.

And then, just above Castle Meadow, there was the fresh tumult of the horse sale.

Half Norwich was like a farmyard on those Saturdays, when cattle and sheep were driven in to market from the farms or from Trowse Station, and then driven out again through the streets to the pastures of their buyers. I remember a wild bullock being chased by a wilder drover out of our school playground and across the headmaster's flower beds, back into the street.

There is nothing quite like that now. Store cattle are rarely brought to market on the speculation of a sale. Fat cattle are collected and graded for the Ministry of Food on

Mondays. Bacon pigs are sent to Birmingham. Sheep have almost disappeared from Norfolk, and horses are well-nigh obsolete. Half the market is already a car park, and nearly all the beasts that come there today are brought by lorry. The market my children see is but the shadow of the one I used to see – yet it is still captivating to them.

They are seeing the last of it; for I suppose it is true that Norwich Hill, with its steep and slippery cobbled slopes, its lack of accommodation for the precious tuberculin-tested dairy cattle, and its cramped space for lorries to be parked, washed and disinfected, cannot be made to meet the requirements of a modern market. Cattle market is becoming more sanitary, a more orderly, and I hope a more humane business than it used to be.

Norwich is hoping to build a market on the new model at Harford Bridges – clean, level, orderly, efficient. It could eventually have model slaughterhouses and a meat packing station adjacent to it. If all goes according to plan it will be the centre of a great revival of the livestock industry of East Anglia, and the old hurly-burly of Norwich Hill will be forgotten.

It was not, of course, a good thing that herds of frightened beasts should be driven through the busiest traffic of the Norwich streets.

An hour on Norwich Hill twenty or thirty years ago might well have converted a sensitive man into a vegetarian, and the sight of muzzled calves nuzzling vainly at the distended udders of their dams might also have caused him to forswear milk as well as veal.

Perhaps I was callous – it is kinder to myself to say I was bemused by the noise and movement of the market and blind to the details.

And yet... And yet, if Norwich Hill could be made as sanitary, orderly and humane as a market ought to be, I believe it would be good for the city if the market could remain there. I believe it is good for the character of Norwich to be reminded, by the weekly presence of the cattle market in its very midst, that all cities depend on agriculture and that one of the prime functions of this city in particular is to be the capital and market of an agricultural province.

Something of the heart will have gone out of Norwich when the people no longer take their children in to see the Cattle Market.

Previous pages: *The cattle market as it was. The site is now the Castle Mall shopping complex.*

The Speedway

September 1958

Eric Fowler

I am old fashioned enough never to have seen until last Saturday a speedway race. I was urged thereto by the vituperations of the critics who, reading that the riders sometimes get hurt and sometimes get killed, and knowing that the races attract large crowds of adolescents, consider the speedway an unpleasant and sinister phenomenon, comparable to the gladiatorial games of ancient Rome, if not to the feeding of lions with Christians. Having now seen the speedway, I recommend these critics also to go and see. I predict that although they may become a little bored towards the end of the evening they will not be profoundly shocked.

One very striking thing about it was certainly the youth of the crowd. There were about 10,000 of them, standing on an embankment round an oval track. The surface of the track was of red grit, known by the initiates as shale. In the centre was greensward, and on the outside of the red track was a stout wooden fence, about four feet high and painted white. Schoolboys hung upon this fence, and I noticed that they all possessed one or other of the accoutrements of a motor-cyclist in imitation of the heroes of the track. One would have a leather helmet, another gauntlets; and even the poorest or least enterprising boys had cellulose eyeshields, sold off cheap as surplus military stores, and serving them as goggles. Behind them were ranked hundreds of youths and girls who I should guess were just starting work in factories and shops, or on the land, and who wore, as tokens of their devotion to the speedway, scarves in the colours of the local team. It was in great part a country crowd, for the gabble of Norwich was equally matched with the broader accent of the countryman.

The affair was ceremonious, and expertly organised. A procession of six ambulance men in black and a dozen attendants in white overalls, bearing long scrapers to smooth the surface of the track, stepped out under the floodlights to a march tune and took up their allotted stations around the oval. A loud speaker announced that a rider who had had 15 stitches taken out of his injured foot the previous Wednesday would race again the following Saturday, and that another rider, a favourite, who it was apprehended had broken his collar bone a week ago, would race this evening. It occurred to me that the management of the speedway did not minimise the hardihood of its riders or the risks attendant on their calling, and that it perhaps provoked criticism by its own propaganda.

The attendants brought four motor cycles, stripped to the bare essentials of a frame, two wheels and an engine, and placed them at the starting point. The four riders came out, visored like the knights of old and clad from helmeted head to iron clad foot in leather. On their cuirasses they bore the blazonry of their teams – green-and-yellow for Norwich, red-and-white for their opponents. They looked like something between medieval knights and the popular idea of men from Mars. They were dehumanised by their armour, but the crowd knew them and shouted their names.

They mounted their machines, and, two to each rider, the white-clad attendants

Speedway at The Firs in Norwich, home to The Stars.

pushed them forward till the engines started. They made a preliminary circuit of the track, then, with engines roaring, they lined up behind the starting gate. The gate clashed upwards like an inverted guillotine, and with a great noise from the engines and a great shout from the crowd the riders shot forward, their machines swerving and skidding beneath them as the wheels sought a grip on the track. They came to the first corner in a line, and went into four diagonal skids, each rider pivoting himself and his machine on an outstretched left foot. There were sparks beneath the iron-shod boots, and from the rear wheel of each machine rose a dark plume of shale, which fell in a cascade on the white fence and among the crowd, who accepted it as an honourable baptism. A red-and-white cuirass held the inside of the first bend and hurtled towards the second, with two green-and-yellows neck-and-neck in pursuit and the other red-and-white thundering in the rear. The leader took the inside of the second bend, then swung perilously far out, until he all but touched the fence. At the third bend, the leading green-and-yellow stole the inner place, and then he was past, and sliding round the fourth bend and into the second lap, while the crowd yelled "Paddy! Good old Paddee-ee!" The paladin or Martian, thus humanised as Paddy roared ahead, while behind him his comrade of the green-and-yellow fought with the opposing champion of the red-and-white, a furious battle of horse-power and man-power for second place.

The winner covered four laps of a 425-yard track with four bends in it at an average speed of about 45 miles an hour. The stink of burnt motor fuel was acrid, the din was infernal, and the crowd loved it, yelling encouragement to Paddies and Teds and Tommies and Freds who, absorbed and deafened in their perilous game, could not have heard a word that was shrieked to them. Once a rider for the red-and-white touched the fence and fell, but he fell as cleverly as he rode, the others as skilfully swerved past him, and he rolled clear, unhurt – neither could I make out that anybody in the crowd thirsted for his blood. Rather did they gasp with relief.

There were 14 races of two against two, and in the end the green-and-yellow riders won by 54 points to 29, which was too great a margin for the latter races to be interesting. Or, at any rate, they were not interesting to me. For all the admirable skill and hardihood of the riders, I began to detect a certain similarity and even monotony about the succession of races. I could not sustain my enthusiasm as the children of the machine age who stood around me, surging up to the fence, and eager, after the last race was over, for the triumphal parade, when the riders rode slowly round the track with helmets and visors removed, and Paddy, the most formidable of the machine-men, played the clown for the benefit of the crowd, and stood revealed as a little fellow with a most engaging Irish grin.

I could perceive no element of blood lust nor much of hysteria in this sport. It is, of course, a dangerous sport, but I doubt whether it is more dangerous than steeple-chasing, against which there is no outcry. In a commercial sport, run quite frankly for the profit of the proprietors of the tracks, and as such is perhaps unworthy of the youthful loyalties it engages, but the same might be said of any other sport run primarily to attract gate-money – and at any rate this is not a gamblers sport. This crowd comes to watch and enthuse, but not to bet. And it is not unnatural that children of the machine-age should be interested in a sport that makes use of machines. They are enthralled, as perhaps their elders are not, by noise and speed but for their admiration, at the root, is for the daring of the riders, and whatever you may think of commercialised sport – speedway riders are perhaps more healthily objects for hero-worship than film stars.

Cock Canaries and Mad Hatters

March 1959

Eric Fowler

On the second visit of Norwich City to White Hart Lane, one was inclined to take it as an established function of the borough of Tottenham that all its streets should be car parks for vehicles decorated with yellow and green ribbons, and its pavements promenades for crowds wearing yellow and green favours and speaking broad Norfolk.

But, entering at the rear of the three-decker grandstand half an hour before the match and climbing flight after flight of concrete stairs, I began to fear that I had mistaken the time. From the cheering, and the roars of "On the ball City!" it sounded as if the game had already started and Norwich City were pressing the defence hard. Emerging into my seat on the top deck of that mountain of a grandstand, I found that it was all right – the noise was merely the Norwich supporters clearing their throats.

A military band was playing in the middle of the football pitch. It was inaudible – except that from time to time, in a lull in the cheering and singing, the thump of the drums made itself faintly heard. Two massed choirs of maybe ten thousand members, at either end of the ground, were at different stages of the chorus "On the ball City!" They were being encouraged by twenty transplanted citizens of Norwich – known as mascots – who were parading the cinder track around the football pitch, dressed from head to foot in yellow and green, in the likeness of Norwich canaries, Norfolk dumplings, and mad costermongers on the way to a yellow and green Derby.

It was some time before one recollected that a team from Luton were also involved in this affair, that their colours were black and white, and that they were known as the Hatters. It was then possible, after careful scrutiny, to pick out among the overwhelming yellow and green on the terraces, many patches of black and white favours and white straw hats with black ribbons. Five Luton mascots were doing their valiant best to equal the efforts of twenty Norwich rivals. One of them, giving a passable imitation of an American cheer-leader, was leading the black and white part of the crowd in rhythmic shouts of "L-U-T-O-N," to the accompaniment of a furious ringing of handbells. But I believe that even if he had had a corps of drum-majorettes to help him, the answering chorus of "On the ball City!" would still have swamped the best efforts of the Luton supporters. For they, to their undoing, had no anthem.

Nevertheless, it turned out that when the match began that they had an excellent football team. Above all, they had a little forward named Bingham, who wove his way down the right wing like a will-o'-the-wisp, but demonstrated, whenever he got within range of goal, that he could also kick like a mule.

Bingham had the veteran Norwich captain, Ashman, beaten for speed, but not, fortunately, for knowledge of tactics. And against the efforts of Bingham's colleagues to convert his passes into goals, Butler, the tall Norwich centre-half, and Kennon, the goalkeeper, performed prodigies of football valour, while the wiry young Thurlow, at right-back, attended competently to the other wing.

There are two kinds of goalkeeper – the inconspicuous but steadfast, and the spectacular. To an anxious and highly partisan spectator like myself, the inconspicuous sort of goalkeeper is the more comforting. Kennon – to whom has fallen the nerve-racking job of replacing the injured Nethercott at the most critical stage of the cup-ties – is of the spectacular kind. He is a huge and handsome South African. Any ball that trespasses inside the penalty area is his, and he hurls himself at it like a charging lion. Once he has got it, he can throw it, accurately, as far as the half-way line, or kick it, if necessary, the length of the field. He is not only the last line of defence. He looks like part of the attack.

However, for most of the first half Norwich were forced on to the defensive. After half an hour I began to wonder how many more corner kicks Luton could possibly force without scoring, and at length they got their goal – not, as it happened, from a corner, but from a lobbed centre from Bingham, which the Scottish international, Brown, headed home with superb accuracy. Neither Kennon or any other goalkeeper could have been blamed for failing to reach that one, and the shout that went up for the first time showed how many Luton spectators there were.

Norwich fought back against the most competent defence they have yet encountered. The sage Owen, at centre-half, had such an understanding with his goalkeeper, Baynham, that between them they could always prevent those electrifying swoops of Bly – whether upon Ashman's through-passes down the middle of the ground, or Brennan's delicately judged chip-shots from the left wing.

The swift, sturdy Crossan, on the right, threatened to become a Norwich counterpart to Bingham. But at the expense of severe censure from the referee, the Luton left-back – less scrupulous than Ashman – checked Crossan's speed by sheer force. What, with one thing and another, the first half was Luton's, and at half-time the chorus of Norwich spectators was so muted that it was at last possible to hear what the Tottenham military band was playing.

The band marched off, and Norwich came out for the second half determined, as it seemed, to do or die. Hitherto they had lacked that extra yard of dash that had won their previous matches, and the wing half-backs could not assert their former dominance. But now the passes began to find their men; and within five minutes the crew-cut head of Crossan had sped the ball like a bullet into the net. The Norwich roar rose again, full-throated, only to be checked, sickeningly, as the referee disallowed the goal – someone, it seemed, had obstructed the goalkeeper before the ball reached Crossan.

But this team, as it has shown before, has the courage to fight adversity. After fifteen minutes more of struggle, a long pass across the field from McCrohan found Brennan unmarked.

Brennan, as footballers go, is an old stager. In its more relaxed moments the crowd had been reminding him by singing "Happy birthday to you," that the day was his 35th birthday. One has regarded him, latterly, as more of a goal-maker for young thrusters like Bly and Crossan than a goal-scorer. But he took that pass from McCrohan as the most acceptable of birthday presents, gathered it, steadied himself, and sent a shot like a rocket past the desperate finger-tips of Baynham.

Now the Norwich roar swelled, unchecked, and "On the ball City!" urged the team on to the kill and the Cup Final.

But Luton, too, were stung into fresh efforts, and Crowe, that usually classic left-half, showed the first sign of nerves on the Norwich side when, despairing of stopping Bingham by any other means, he took him in his arms and embraced him. The intention, clearly, was more bear-like than brotherly, and the referee duly pointed out that this was

Tottenham and not Twickenham.

Thenceforward the balance of the game swung from end to end of the field like a pendulum, carrying the spectators' thumping hearts with it.

It was appropriate that the last act was a magnificent leap into mid-air by Kennon, to save a point-blank from Bingham, who had sailed clean through the Norwich defence in a final attempt to win the match for Luton on his own. And so the tens of thousands in yellow and green departed – their minds already preparing fresh intrigues for the time, money and tickets for the replay at Birmingham.

Norwich City's Terry Allcock clashes with the Luton goalkeeper during the FA Cup semi-final at White Hart Lane in 1959. The game, played in front of 63,500 supporters, ended in a 1-1 draw, Brennan scoring City's goal. The Canaries lost the replay 1-0, in front of a crowd of 49,500 at St Andrews, Birmingham.

Touched by the colours of sunset

November 1960

Eric Fowler

There was an evening last week when I stood at a high window and watched the towers, trees and roofs of Norwich darken beneath a sky flecked with high clouds, still tinted with rose and gold by the light of the sun that had just sunk below the horizon.

A friend at my elbow quoted "Born of the day that died, the eve, now dying, sank to rest". Later on, when the clouds would turn pale and misty, and the sky black, we should see the slender white shaft of the cathedral spire, floodlit, above the neighbouring roofs.

That evening was the beginning of the second summer of the year – the first having been almost forgotten during the intervening rains of July and August.

At the weekend, when we went down to the sea to revel in the sun, we saw combine harvesters still busy in the fields even on Sunday, getting in the rest of the corn.

The farmers could not trust the summer to return for long; yet still it lingers into autumn.

Mindful of the kindly sunset that shone its promise on the clouds, I have been strolling about Norwich in these golden days, enjoying the painted colours that have spread for three or four years past along the city streets, rather like the colours of the sunset creeping gradually across the sky.

I think it was the painting – somewhat after the style of a Suffolk village – of the old plaster-fronted houses in Elm Hill that started the glow that has crept across Norwich. Possibly it goes further back, to the fresh paint and window boxes into which the city burgeoned for the Festival of Britain in 1951.

Or it may even date back to the inspiration, when the City Hall was built, of covering all the market stalls with coloured tilts. At all events the Civic Trust's work in Magdalen Street pursued the trend, popularised it, and more elaborately originated a system whereby shopkeepers happily conspire with architects to glorify the decoration of whole streets.

Now from Magdalen Street it has spread to the wonderful jumble of building of all styles and periods that surround the Market Place.

There is a splendid 17th century house at the corner of White Lion Street, whose occupation by the True-Form Company was for long said to bely the name, since the conflicting advertisements of multiple tenants had sadly deformed it.

Now the several tenants, collaborating in the redecoration, have pulled the old house back into shape, and exhibited it, for the first time in living memory, as the fine building it is.

The Queen Anne house at the bottom of Guildhall Hill, likewise deformed, is about to be put back into shape by similar co-operation. Victorian buildings, previously written off as dull if not downright ugly, today stand out as interesting characters.

And the one new building on the Walk – Philips and Dolcis – falls most gracefully into harmony with its neighbours of the Regency.

It is our most distinguished example of modern shop design, and a far greater ornament than any new building which, in a mistaken conception of what constitutes good taste in an old city, is disguised in an old fashioned style. It even gives rise to a hope that we may be on the verge of a reform of our architecture as well as our decoration.

From the Walk the colour is beginning to run, joyously, into the Haymarket, Davey Place and London Street – and from Guildhall Hill up into St Giles'. It breaks out again in Swan Lane and Bridewell Alley. St Benedict's is being provoked into rivalry with Magdalen Street; and from Magdalen Street, moreover, the new decoration is starting to move into Wensum Street and up Tombland.

Neither is that all. If you go to the outskirts and look at the housing estates you will see that new painting is doing all that bright colour can do to relieve the monotony which is perhaps inseparable from the mass-building of dormitories.

And there are still hopes that the Corporation may yet be inspired to regard the great Heartsease Estate as the new township it really is, and build a heart into it. For Norwich Corporation is like the young Queen Victoria – it does try to be good.

But, coming back to the centre, there are, of course, limits to the extent to which new paint can be used to qualify architecture. Now that it is too late, everyone says what a pity it is that Orford Place has been rebuilt as Awful Place and we are left wondering whether better can be done about the upper half of St Stephen's, which has yet to be reconstructed – and what is going to happen about the surroundings of the old cattle market, and Ber Street and King Street, and poor, picturesque, dilapidated Coslany. It might be more optimistic not to compare the new colours of Norwich to a sunset, but to think of them hopefully as the possible precursors of a sunrise in a modern architecture.

Finally – since a man must have a grouse, even in the midst of the unexpected enjoyment of a second summer – I find myself shocked every time I come into Norwich from outside it by those immodest road signs that welcome the visitor to a Fine City. If I were a visitor, I should prefer to draw my own conclusions.

These signs are not worthy of a county that has so many more modest and beautiful local signs in its villages and country towns. Surely the better practice is the general one, of erecting at the entrances to a city a sign embellished with its coat of arms, and simply announcing its name. The design and lettering should bespeak the quality of the place.

In the market for a fair

Autumn 1961

Eric Fowler

There is some doubt today as to how much longer the Christmas and Easter Fairs on the Old Cattle Market at Norwich will last.

The showmen contend that, although the market has moved to the outskirts of the city, the fairs and their historic site in the centre are still protected by the charters originally granted to the medieval trade fairs on Tombland.

There are other people who point out that the medieval fairs were primarily mercantile. They doubt whether, when it comes to the change of the use of an important site of the middle of the prosperous modern city Norwich has become, the interests of a pleasure fair can prevent new developments.

It may be that in years to come we shall remember the fairs, whirling away beneath the Castle, just as we remember the Cattle Market – as something very picturesque in the life of old Norwich, which lasted until the second half of the twentieth century before it was decided that it was an anachronism in the heart of a modern city.

At any rate, I have ensured that all of my sons will remember it, because on Saturday I took the youngest, at the age of three, to be introduced to the tradition. It was very cold. In my recollection, Norwich fairs, whether at Christmas or Easter, are always cold. Three-year-old was warm enough, in his duffle coat with a furry hood, and his eyes sparkled at the lights and the noise. But when I tried to remember what the fair was like when I was his age, it seemed nearly as new to me as to him.

The latest and fastest thing in the fair of my childhood was a steam roundabout with gilded cars in the likeness of jet aeroplanes, which made howling noises as they swung their passengers up into the air and then brought them swooping down again.

All the roundabouts were dizzier and noisier than ever, and all the steel arms, whirling high in the air, were a blaze of coloured lights in the dusk of the winter afternoon.

Three-year-old was not frightened. He is growing up in a noisy, fast, dangerous, mechanical world. Seeking roundabouts suitable for his age, I could find only one of the old hand-cranked circles of wooden horses.

Elsewhere the showmen, deprived of exercise by electric motors, shivered in the arctic wind, and three-year-old, rosy in his warm hood, rode with aplomb in toy motor cars, and drove a toy motor bus, while two other passengers, even younger, rode in the back and rang the bell. Parents stamped their feet on the cobbles, and beamed at their offspring, riding gravely round and round.

While I was watching, I became conscious that the fair did not even smell as it used to. When I was a little boy it smelt of steam engines, orange peel, and gunpowder from the shooting galleries, with an underlying country aroma of cattle from the market.

Now, it smelt overpoweringly of fried onions; for not only was the mechanised music American, but nearly all the refreshment stalls were given over to the delicacy of hot dogs. I saw only one that still bravely sold toffee apples.

Three-year-old by this time was persuaded that it was time to go home for tea, but going home in itself was an adventure – for, slipping away from the bright lights of the fair on to the dark footpath below the Castle, and then crossing Castle Meadow, we came into Davey Place, roofed with coloured lights. Then we walked over the Market Place, squeezing between the crowds of shoppers, and past the men with bunches of mistletoe, shouting: "Only eighteen pence a spray! You're unlucky if you don't have one in the house. Only eighteen pence a spray!"

Behind them were piles of Christmas trees, bundles of holly, tiers of chrysanthemums: and, along every alley between the stalls, the stacks of fruit looked as if they had been put there as much for decoration as for sale. We came out near the Guildhall, and saw the narrows of Goat Lane roofed, like Davey Place, with coloured lights, and all the shop windows of the Walk and London Street aglow.

Somewhere in that direction, we could hear a band playing: "Hark, the Herald Angels Sing". The clock on the floodlit tower of the City Hall showed it was time we were home, but still we lingered. How could we help it, when the great Christmas tree on the steps of the City Hall, awaiting its carollers, was swaying its branches in the wind, waving all its coloured lights?

Beyond, the windows of St Peter Mancroft were alight. There was another Christmas tree in the archway beneath the tower, and the massive tower itself was floodlit – yellow light for the stonework, and white light for the cupola that shone across the sky, where black clouds were piling up as if for snow.

I thought to myself that in spite of all innovations there was still magic in Norwich at Christmas time – and some new devices, like flood-lighting, civic Christmas trees, and coloured lights strung across the streets had even deepened the spell. It is fun for children to be brought up in a city like this, and still to wake up on Christmas morning, as I did all those years ago, to the sound of St Peter's bells.

The newspaper caption for this 1961 photograph says it all: 'The Norwich Easter Fair opened last night with all its bright lights, loud music and side-shows which tempt you to part with your money. Here young people enjoy themselves on the "dodg'em cars", an old favourite at the fairground.'

11

The changing climate

May 1965

Ralph Mottram

Our climate is changing. I hasten to add, for the better. I might never have known if I had not heard the late W.G.Clarke, surely one of the wisest men who ever wrote for the Eastern Daily Press, explaing to the group who used to gather around him:

"The earth rotates, like a football. That's how we get our dates and times, our seasons and weather. But like a football which has had a glancing kick, it does not rotate regularly. It wobbles!" We didn't grasp what he was driving at, while he added:

"The axis is wobbling towards us. If this motion continues... of course, it may not... but if it does, the polar ice cap may come down as far as Newcastle!"

I suppose we looked alarmed, for he added: "It will take about 15,000 years. So you needn't worry!"

It is not hard to check what Clarke was talking about. For instance: the zone in which grapes will ripen to make wine, has moved steadily south. Old vine stubs have been dug up at Ditchingham in Norfolk, and Bury St Edmunds in Suffolk. I have spoken to Frenchmen who remember when wine, called "Picardin", was made in Picardy, as it is no longer.

But the process is not so simple as that. The very gradual tilting of which Clarke spoke, seems to have made our local climate less extreme, rather than colder. It is true that we no longer hear of the great heats and droughts that are recorded in many old memories and histories. Against this, we have to go a long way back, a century in fact, in a compilation such as Mackie's Annals, to find an entry that describes skating from Norwich to Yarmouth.

This, again, brings in the question of evidence. How much of the freedom of our rivers from ice is the result of better care of the channel, and its use by heavier, power-driven craft? The average person only notices vagaries of climate when they incommode him.

Memorable crises in our local weather are, naturally, likely to be floods. The last to affect Norwich, will be recalled by readers of over fifty years of age. It occured as a result of a gale and cloudburst among the Yare-Wensum valley on Monday, August 26, 1912. Torrential rain burst hundreds of culverts along by-roads, and during the following 24 hours, the mean level of the river, as it flows through Norwich, rose 16 and a half feet. A plaque next to St.George's bridge marks the spot at which the violence of this mass of water was most obvious.

Concerned for the welfare of the caretaker of the Martineau Memorial Hall in Colegate, I went down on my bicycle. The bridge, an erection of the celebrated Sir John Sloane, was shuddering like a living creature in a fit. I was subsequently told by the late Stanley Wearing, that had not the stones been securely "dowelled" into each other by steel pegs, it might have collapsed. The wall of the Norwich Mercury press, immediately west, did so.

However, I took my chance, and north of the bridge had to cycle through a foot of water. Boats were out in Colegate. Heigham Street and Fishergate were awash. Roberts

& Co. issued later a pamphlet, the photographs in which showed that the only people who enjoyed the experience were school children who paddled.

For the housewife in the districts submerged, it was no joke. A flood in a closely built-up area means floating sewage in living rooms. Nor was it a joke for transport authorities. The bridges at Trowse and Lakenham Cock collapsed, as did the Ostrich Inn on Kett's Hill.

From my bedroom in Bracondale, I surveyed a stretch of water that reached from Thorpe church to that at Whitlingham. I watched a boat sail across the Cromer and Yarmouth railway. Water appeared in the Cathedral cloisters, but not the nave, which I believe stands on a "raft". Fortunately there was no loss of human life, though grazing animals were marooned, and the cost of the damage was, by the standards of those days, considerable.

The other "freak of nature" which only those of my age will remember, was the brief but disastrous gale of Sunday, March 24th, 1895. It arose, without warning, at 2pm. My brother and I heard the unusual rumble in the great old chimneys of the Bank House. Glancing outside, we saw hats, bonnets, newspapers flying about 20 feet above Bank Street. Tiles crashed down in all directions, London Street was closed as dangerous.

Next day, the Eastern Daily Press gave the details of an "Enormous destruction." "Cyclone force" prevailed for two to three hours. Over wide areas of Norfolk gable ends and garden walls came crashing down. Unthank Road Chapel (on the Scottish Church site), the Workhouse Chapel, St Augustine's Infants' School (now the Swimming Baths) were damaged. Several of the great elms on Newmarket Road were felled (those planted to replace them, show it by their lesser size). In some parks, cedars that had stood for centuries were torn down. Possibly their foliage made them vulnerable?

This is what can happen. Fortuantely the dates are well dispersed, and wartime memories make Nature's fits seem paltry.

The Cathedral

October 1967

Eric Fowler

On five afternoons a week and twice on Sundays there is a work of art to be heard in the east end of Norwich Cathedral. The singing of the daily services from the Book of Common Prayer is a continuation of what the Benedictine monks, who ministered in the Cathedral before the Reformation, called the Opus Dei. It does not matter whether there is a congregation of twelve people or twelve hundred. The English of Cranmer's prayer book and the James I bible will be just as impressively read, the psalms and anthems just as beautifully sung, because clergy and choir are exercising their art for the glory of God – just as I believe the Cathedral itself, whatever the faults of the men who built it, was built to the glory of God. Not that I think the proud Norman founder, Herbert de Losinga, was unmindful of his own glory, but that was something that lasted no longer than his lifetime.

Whether you care for the Cathedral services is, I think, a matter of temperament. I know people to whom this music, chanting and prayer, regardless of the presence or absence of a congregation, seems as vain as the Buddhist practice of setting prayer wheels to be turned by the wind. The purpose of worship for them is congregational. They see no point in services in which a congregation does not participate by singing heartily, by saying the prayers out loud, and by listening to the exhortations of a preacher. But we have, I hope, gone past the time when people quarrelled and fought about forms of worship as bitterly as they do about politics. Forms of worship are as various as human nature itself.

For myself I have never been able to separate sight from sound, or indeed speech from music, in the mystical experience of hearing a cathedral service. To watch the slow procession of choir and clergy, like the border of an illuminated manuscript: to see the colours gradually fade out or the high windows in the apse, as the winter afternoon turns to dusk; to follow the music with eyes as well as hearing, as it soars from the lit choir stalls into the dimness of the great round arches beneath the tower; to hear the Bible read as the Dean reads it, with a sense of the cadences as well as the forcible meaning of the 17th century prose: to listen to the singing so carefully disciplined and trained that it sounds artless – it is all one. The words, the music and the piled and sculptured stone are blended together, in man's expression of himself as a spiritual being.

Afterwards, I do not want to talk. I want to go away quietly into the dark. But I may, later on, go into the pub for a drink and a gossip, for I am of the earth, earthly. The Cathedral is the nearest I get to mysticism, and then it is a solitary exultation. Writing about it is a result of having gone last Sunday to a service sung by way of thanksgiving for the work of Dr Heathcote Statham, who as organist and master of the choristers has devoted himself for 37 years to glorifying the worship of the Cathedral with music. As conductor of the Philharmonic Society for 33 seasons, and associate conductor of four Norwich Festivals, he has served secular music also: it has been like the Church fulfilling, through this devout musician, her ancient function as a patron and exemplar of the arts.

Dr Statham's compositions, chiefly of church music, will live after him to show prosperity how fine an artist he was. His music is virile and often joyous. The service on Sunday was sung entirely to music of his composition.

With a lesser man, that might have meant risking monotony, but this service, on the contrary, was inspiring.

The service ended with his Rhapsody on a Ground Bass, for the organ, rolling and rejoicing round the Cathedral. Some like their religion plain; others like it coloured: but, plain or coloured, I am sure the worst service that can be done to religion is to take out the poetry and the joy. I do not believe that to make it modern we must make it drab, and rewrite the Bible in Gobbledegook. Let the Church continue to show us the glory of God; for the humanists leave us very short of glory.

Peace and violence

November 1968

Eric Fowler

It was borne in upon me on Remembrance Day, not only that it was the fiftieth anniversary of the end of the first world war, but that it is 23 years since the second world war. This country has now enjoyed – if that is the right word – the longest period of relative peace it has ever had in my lifetime, or that of anyone under the age of 75.

The term peace, of course, is strictly relative to a state of total war. I was only five years old when the first world war broke out, and consequently remember very little of the period before 1914; when, according to most accounts of it, war was the business of professional soldiers and sailors, and civilians, however alarmed they might be about war overseas, did not feel personally involved, as potential cannon-fodder, or victims of air raids or nuclear bombs.

Edwardian England, in spite of the sufferings of the "submerged tenth" of the population from poverty, slums and unemployment, seems to have felt peaceful and prosperous. Even veteran socialists have admitted to me that it did. Nobody has ever felt the same since 1918.

In my boyhood the country was full of disabled men, widows and orphans of the war. On November 11th the widows came out again in their black weeds, leading their orphan children by the hand. The ex-Servicemen paraded in hundreds. Everything stopped, whether it was a working day or not, for the two minutes' silence. Norwich Market Place and all the neighbouring pavements were packed with people. Only two things break the silence. One was the flapping of the wings of the pigeons and the other was the barking of dogs, alarmed by the sudden quiet that had fallen on the city.

It was the same on market places and village greens throughout the country. There was scarcely a family that had not been bereaved by the four years of trench warfare, or hamlet that had not erected its stone memorial to the fallen. We believed, or tried to believe, they had sacrificed themselves in a war to end war.

Then, as now, there were people who felt that processions with military bands and marching troops, and the pomp of civic ceremony, were an incongruous way of commemorating the tragedy of the world war in the hope of world peace. But nobody was churl enough to interrupt. It was and still is the best way survivors know to commemorate the deaths of their comrades, and their hopes of "a world fit for heroes to live in."

And as to that new world, it was pervaded during my young manhood by the further tragedy of mass unemployment, and by the growth in Russia, Germany and Italy of dictatorships that ruled by force and glorified war – either class war or nationalist and racial war.

By the time I was in my twenties it was impossible for anybody who was not wilfully blind to deny the likelihood of another war. The harder we tried to believe it would not happen, the more we were deceiving ourselves. I had as a friend and colleague one of those characters who enjoyed military life. He had been a cavalry man in Mesopotamia, and he used to mock the old men – when they lamented lower taxes and cheaper prices they had before 1914 – by saying, “I wore out five horses that you paid for, thank you very much!”

Then he used to turn on us young men and say, “next time I shall sit at home and pay for your tanks.” But when the next time came, in 1939, he could not bear to be out of it. He wrangled his way into service with the R.A.F., that took him into every theatre of war from Europe to the Far East and back again.

The chief difference between my generation, that took part in the second world war, and the older generation that fought in the first, is that thanks to the warnings of our elders we went into it with few illusions. Because it was a war of movement, we were at least spared the holocaust of trench warfare. At the end – consciously or unconsciously regarding the second war as a continuation of the first – we erected no new memorials. We simply appended the names of the fallen of 1939-45 to those of 1914-18 – and, mercifully, the lists were shorter.

Since 1945 another generation has grown up in England that has never known war: although, thanks to the speed and vividness of modern communications, it has been impressed with the horrors of war wherever it has continued to be fought. At the same time it has enjoyed greater domestic security – freedom from want – than its elders ever knew. To that extent, the survivors of 1939-45 were not cheated as their predecessors were.

It is this new generation on whose behalf we are urged to abandon the whole ceremony of Remembrance Day, on the grounds either that it means nothing to them or that, if it means anything, it means a glorification of war. The younger generation – or at any rate the most politically active of them – exercise their instinct to march by marching on Trafalgar Square or the American Embassy on Sunday afternoons, and express their detestation of warfare by assaulting London policemen.

At the same time there is such a wave of crime sweeping the country – theft, insensate destruction and violence – as we have never known before. It is as if there is an instinct for violence in mankind which, if denied an outlet in warfare, breaks out into malice against domestic law and order. I believe that those who decry the spectacle of Remembrance Day are in fact envious of it. Having denied the old, however limited, the virtues of patriotism, loyalty and self discipline, they have found nothing to put in their place. We have, so far, failed to evoke these qualities in the service of peace, but we badly need to do so.

The days of old labour

December 1970

Adrian Bell

My opening speech failed me. I could only say "Look at all these handles. Do you see how thin they are worn, how shiny they are? No French polish, no patent lacquer, could give them that surface. Only generations of hands turning, turning, for ever turning. Turning for us before we were born."

I was opening a rural museum of old farm tools.

"Think of those men and women who turned all these handles, for hours and days and years, that we might stand here fed and clothed. Superhuman feats will men do to win a cup, but nobody raised a cheer for these, or ever said 'Well done!'"

I can't forget those handles, for I myself when a youth had turned for hours at a time nearly every handle represented in that collection. But one at a time and at intervals. It was the sight of them there all together and worn so thin, even gracefully thin, which brought it home to me.

It had been a salutary shock to me having just left a posh school at the age of 18, and gone on a farm, to find myself equated with the village idiot.

I could have gone to Cambridge and been regarded as a brain, but here I was set to turn a handle. It was all I was good for in the nicely ordered combination of skills whereby food was produced 50 years ago.

Here my education counted for nothing, and most of it was nothing, I slowly came to realise as I turned the handle of the seed dressing machine in the barn all day.

The handle activated a number of wire sieves which shook from side to side, and beaters which revolved and blew the chaff away. It also blew away with the chaff half the things that up to that time I had thought important to my knowledge of life.

The next week I and the village simpleton (employed for a pittance on such jobs) took it in turns to turn the handles for the cake crusher and the root pulper.

In the dairy the missis and her maid were taking it in turns to turn the handle of the butter churn.

There was another machine, which was furnished with two handles, and was still sometimes used – a chaff-cutter in the loft above the stable. I and Silly Billy also co-operated in turning this when the horsekeeper wanted some hay chaffed.

One did a lot of this turning before one was considered fit even to touch the handles of a plough, handles which needed a control far more adroit than the simple act of turning.

Sheer drudgery it was. Yes, but also a sweating out of former notions. After the first rebelliousness at being regarded as equal in labour value only to Silly Billy, I got to know him for a trustful and affectionate youth.

I got to know the sounds of the work being done, as if they were familiar voices. There was the complicated judder of the dressing machine, as the plump seed beans came spilling out in a heap on the barn floor.

There was the moist, crisp noise that the root-slicer made which muted to a fractious "ch-ch" when a root got jammed.

There was the sloshy sound of the cream in the end-over-end churn, changing to a "thump-thump" as the butter came.

As a holiday from the handles, the farmer I worked under took me to the Christmas fatstock sale at Bury St Edmunds. There, as I was gazing at a fat hog, a farmer spoke to me.

He was 89, he told me, and had been born a labourer's son. In his youth he had seen 20 men walking to the workhouse in December, and their wives and children following in a waggon.

But his father had a good master, a man who, seeing men standing round the blacksmith's fire one day towards Christmas, asked them why they stood idle.

"Because we haven't any work, master, nor anything to eat neither, or a bit of firing in our housen," they replied.

He told them to go to his door, and they would be given bread and bacon, and when they had eaten he would give them work to do.

"Everybody in this parish must have a Christmas dinner," he said.

The old farmer told me this so simply, along with the terrible picture of the families going to spend Christmas in the workhouse, that it sounded almost like some verses out of the Bible.

When I got back, I wrote it down just as he spoke it. Years later, writing a book on farm life, I included it. It filled just a page. It is the best page in the book, and it was not my writing at all, but that man speaking, a horsekeeper's son who had left school when he was about 12 years old.

It still moves me to read it, because that man spoke so naturally, without conscious art; it was his life.

And it is literature. When today's pundits speak of Culture, I just wonder what it is they think they are talking about.

Some harvest festivals

October 1971

Adrian Bell

From Monday to Saturday this lane has a traffic of farm machines; but on a fine Sunday in October it becomes a little blackberry festival. Cars are tucked into gateways, and people stand in chosen spots in that patient tip-toe attitude of the blackberry-picker, often with a handkerchief draped over one hand to staunch the flesh wounds of thorns.

Character appears even in blackberrying. Some devote themselves to one spot and pick a basketful: others wander up and down, peeking and peering, with a vague feeling that bounty is somewhere else, and pick only half a basket in the same time. Myself I am something between these two types. It is understood that my wife is doing the serious picking: she sees beyond the blackberries to what they are to become – jelly or pie or bottled fruit.

Every blackberry I see looks smaller than it should when I come to pick it: there is some place where they are bigger, riper. My wife recalls wonderful blackberries in Dorset when she was a girl, but wastes no time in looking for such in East Anglia, but picks what are here and praises them for what they are.

I do settle in a little while to my favourite game, which is trying to pick blackberries that are out of reach. They hang there up against the sky, rich clusters of them, and big – surely bigger for being up there above the crowd and in full sun.

"Don't tear yourself looking for the unobtainable," she advises. "There are lots of good ones under your hand." But not such good ones, I am sure, and I thrust into the bush and reach up my stick, crook first, and hook towards me a high and laden shoot.

After an afternoon of doing this, when I saw a picture of the new Bishop after his enthronement blessing his diocese, I could only think what a particularly good blackberry-snatcher his long plain Episcopal shepherd's crook would be. He could have reached down clusters beyond my range. As I helped fill my wife's basket, I realised that only in the country is our language still real: "by hook or by crook" was no metaphor. Roadside blackberries pay the farmer no dividends, but they are a bonus to town-dwellers. Eyes whose daily view is only wall, pavements and plate glass, when focused for an afternoon on a hedge, absorb a variety of wild nature beyond the blackberries that occupy the fingers.

A pasture lately ploughed has been manured and cultivated during the dry month just past. I asked a neighbour who happened also to be picking blackberries with his family what was going to be planted on it. "Blackberries," he replied. Himalayan blackberries, the cultivated sort, described in my nurseryman's catalogue as "enormous in growth, prolific in fruit".

It would have seemed strange to our ancestors that a time should come when blackberries should command a better return per acre than the staff of life that they had grown. They could not have foreseen breeds of wheat that should yield twice the weight of grain of even such latter-day varieties as Yeoman, or Squarehead's Master. What chance would such wheat stand today?

Norfolk reed thatcher Fred Cossey putting new thatch on to a cottage being restored at Woodbastwick, continuing the tradition of thatched buildings in this part of the village – including the church. This photograph is from 1986.

Well, a very curious chance, perhaps, in that the straw, say, of Squarehead's Master might be worth more for thatching commuter's country houses than the grain for bread, there being a boom in thatching.

Who could have foreseen that? Not the old boys who lived under those roofs once. "Brick and slate, my boy that's the stuff," my farming tutor often repeated to me when I was 20 years old. Luckily succeeding generations have thought differently, so the old village homes have been preserved and thatchers are busy as never before.

Straw, which most farmers burn, is also a harvest to be thankful for – on a roof. Harvest festivals occur in cities as well as villages. I recall our daughter's indignation that the church in Bournemouth where her school worshipped was equipped with plaster varnished brown.

They had been used to the real thing in our tiny village church – and lots of it. By the time all the produce of the fields was represented inside, we were closely embowered. The vicar, a shortish man, was glimpsed fugitively as he stepped from behind huge sheaves to the lectern, where he was engulfed in maize. The preacher was spectral in the pulpit through barley bristling up around him.

But harvest festival in a country school is becoming almost unique, since there are so few schools in the countryside. The corners of the assembly hall were rounded into hills of flowers and fruits: there were knots of wheat, beatitudes of bread. A consort of recorders descant in the back row, as if it were inhabited by birds, not children. The children did it all: the prayers were of their composing; two by two they brought offerings – a chip basket containing brown eggs nesting in fruiting brambles... The Rector's part was just to give a short address and a blessing.

There was another October festival – of steam and the living horse power. Here in one field were two steam threshing tackles at work, a pair of Suffolk Punches ploughing, veteran tractors, and one shire horse pulling a harvest wagon. Elders sniffed nostalgically the mixture of coal smoke and cereal dust. To us its heyday all seemed so little while ago.

What really held my eyes were the horse and the wagon. It is only when a thing is nearly extinct that you really see it – see that subtle harmony of contradictory movements of four legs, stalking like long black shadows and great wheels slowly revolving. Around and around they crept, giving people rides. Across the hames of the horse-collar were a set of bells. "Klang-klong," they were heard at every pause in the fairground music. "Klang-klong" as the veteran tractors ceased, and the hum of threshing died, and horse and wagon meandered away into the sunset. Our roads must once have been carillons, recognisable perhaps by their owners, even as sheep-bells were.

I recall a passage from Richard Jefferies, of a flock of sheep heard approaching from a distance. "Before we reached the garden gate Hilary turned back, remarking: 'It's Johnson's flock: I know by the tang of his tankards.'"

The American Memorial

July 1975

Eric Fowler

I was trying during the weekend to remember what Norwich looked like when I returned from Burma in October, 1945, at the end of the war. Orford Place was a great hole in the ground, where the basements of the bombed shops had been converted into a water tank for the use of the Fire Brigade in air raids. It also served some bright spirits, the following summer, for a bathing pool. St. Stephen's was a wreck. So was St. Benedicts, and so was the old industrial district north of the river – Over-the-Water, whose reconstruction is now being proudly displayed as Norwich's contribution to the European Architectural Heritage Year.

The big iron pipes of emergency water mains ran along the streets. The brick and concrete tops of air-raid shelters projected across the pavements. There were charred gaps between the houses. Stone walls and pillars were pitted by bomb fragments. Roofs damaged by blast, were a patchwork.

Apart from military trucks and jeeps, the traffic consisted of pre-1940 vehicles, running on strictly rationed petrol. And the people, also strictly rationed both for food and clothing, wore pre-1940 clothes. There was still a lot of khaki in the streets – British battle dress, the smoother American battle dress, and the brown tunics and pink pants of the American walking-out dress. There were patrols of military police – British "redcaps" and American "snowdrops," with their white helmets and nightsticks.

Shabby and in some ways strange as it might be, this was nevertheless home to the returning soldier. Beneath the scars of war I joyously recognised the old familiar city of the white Cathedral spire and the massive Castle keep; the grey church towers rising above crinkly red pantile roofs in the narrow, crooked streets; the great open market place, the gardens, and the trees in the little "plains." Yet, looking out now at the tall office blocks, the supermarts, the widened streets and the perpetual throng of traffic, I find it oddly difficult to remember the Norwich of 1945 – mutilated, poor, bereaved, but happy at the end of six years of war. The change has come upon me gradually over the course of thirty years – and half the present population cannot remember wartime Norwich at all.

It occurred to me at the weekend that Norwich of 1945 is the one that thousands of Americans still remember – some of them perhaps more clearly than I do. For there was a remarkable period in local history that I, in common with others who were overseas, missed.

This was the period 1942-1944, when the U.S.A.A.F. joined the R.A.F. in the assault from the air upon Germany, and the level fields of East Anglia were like one vast airbase. Three hundred thousand of the 8th U.S. Air Force were stationed in Britain. Fifty thousand of the 2nd Air Division, with their headquarters at Ketteringham Hall, just outside Norwich, serviced and flew the great Liberator bombers, which, with their fighter escorts, started their raids from airfields in Norfolk and Suffolk. Six thousand of that division died in the air war that was fought from East Anglia.

Other people have described the Liberators massing, layer upon layer, in droning circles in the Norfolk sky, as they assembled for their raids across the North Sea; the nights broken by the wail of sirens giving warning of German counter-raids, the "rump-rump-rump" of bombs, the bark of anti-aircraft fire; the listening for the return of allied aircraft in groups or singly – some, crippled, to crash in the fields. And there must have been times in 1943 and 1944, off duty, when there were more young Americans than young Englishmen in the Norwich streets.

The 2nd Air Division, before they left in 1945, subscribed a fund of £20,000 and entrusted it to a Norwich board of governors to erect a memorial to their dead. It took eighteen years before Norwich, concentrating on the reconstruction of its industries, house-building and school-building, was able to complete the new central library in which the American memorial was to be incorporated. Meanwhile the 2nd Air Division Association, which had been formed in the U.S. in 1948, waited patiently. They came over in hundreds, in 1963, for the dedication of the memorial at a spectacular and deeply moving service at St. Peter Mancroft Church, and for the opening by the Queen Mother of the American library and reading room in the new library.

Every year they have kept up a supply of books for the library. In 1972 they returned to Norwich for their annual convention. Last week they came back again – over four hundred of them. (They explained that there would have been more but for the currency inflation which has hit America as well as ourselves.) I was privileged to attend their meeting in the Council chamber at the City Hall. Men now grey-haired announced themselves as coming from Pennsylvania or California, Alabama or Michigan, and talked familiarly about Hethel or Rackheath, Bungay or Metfield. They brought gifts of books for the library, medals and pictures for the Norwich collection of Americana, addresses from their home cities to the Lord Mayor.

And the burden of their discussion was extraordinary. They spoke not of a declining but an increasing membership of the Association. They were raising a fund of 50,000 dollars so that the endowment of their memorial should keep pace with the inflation, and the supply of American literature should possibly be extended to other Norfolk libraries. Beyond this, there was talk of approaches to charitable foundations, and of an attempt to raise a much larger sum, which would provide not only for the supply of books to libraries, but for scholarships and for educational travel between England and the United States – "a living memorial" which would outlast its founders and serve future generations.

It was a bold discussion at a time of political, economic and moral stress for both our countries. Underlying it was an anxiety that, whatever plans there might be for an extension of the Trust in the future, nothing should detract from the care of the memorial room in Norwich, which is close to the hearts of the survivors of the 2nd Air Division. I went with one of them to the library. He wanted to look at the fountain in the courtyard, which has, embedded in the bottom of its pool, stones from every state in the Union. He was concerned that one or two of the stones were missing, and wanted them replaced.

There is nothing else quite like this maintenance, by the veterans of the 2nd Air Division, of a memorial in the capital of the English province in which they served. We should be proud of the place East Anglia still holds in their affections. One of them wrote in 1947:

"England gave compensation for the life of combat and work. We lived in the cold of its winter. The peace and beauty of its spring and summer were salted with the bitterness of war. Its people were our friends – though to some they were too like us to be considered foreign, and their tolerance of bad plumbing, cold, and what we thought was lack of progress, did not too much endear them to us."

This was an honest impression, written very close to the time when it was formed. It is heartening now to find that the affection – although not the Norfolk climate – has grown warmer while thirty years have rolled by.

Film actor James Stewart pictured in Norfolk where he was stationed during the second world war. He flew Liberators on bombing missions to Germany.

Overleaf: *Stewart looks at the roll of honour in the American Room at the Central Library, Norwich in 1983. With him is Tom Eaton, the then-chairman of the board of governors of the American Memorial Trust.*

History of houses

November 1975

Adrian Bell

I was one of a hundred people for whom this ancient house had been thrown open for the afternoon, members of the historical society.

Walking through rooms by the acre, reverently feeling the patina of the linenfold panelling, until the hands found themselves simply being used to support the body, as one murmured "wonderful". Drowned in centuries.

It is dazing, for this is only one house which, but for the courtesy of the historical society, I should not have known ever existed. We have already come from one, in which my sister lives: they are going on to yet a third today, which I shall not see. All in one parish.

And there are hundreds, thousands, of such houses still lovingly preserved in this England, which is now more "educated" and more ruthlessly set on beauty's destruction, with or without consent of planner, than at anytime since the harrowing of the north.

Bulldozers, earth-gougers, plough across Constable's Dedham Vale as everywhere. Contractors duly earn knighthoods. Thereafter come litter, broken bottles, transistors.

This blessed plot...

A crowd is a crowd. But no, it's not. Wonderful old tree-nested houses, moats and stewponds coroneted with iris blades, and a hundred people gather there, of whom the question never arises, will they leave any litter? Will they walk about with transistors? They just do not.

Young people, old people, decrepit people. People who simply have to will themselves up those stairs. But up they go, enraptured by the ages. Is that a coupled saltire? Chevron? Quatrefoil?

"The door used to be just there. There will be a screen across the big room inside, I expect." There is a screen.

"The kitchen was a separate building, they carried the dishes across the open and into the hall, then through the two doorways through the screen..."

I begin to see them; clouted pantlers, cooks, bearing boars' heads, suckling pigs, venison pasties, warden pies.

And there once sat in the great hall of this house, banging the board with their drinking horns, those old families with names like Grossemite, Blewtoth, Morieux...

Swords and lutes were in almost equal prestige, when all this decoration came in that was lavished on the heart-of-oak impending over us. We stand under the ribs of the great oak forest that was England.

And then in the 18th century, the age of reason, they hacked the beams to make a grip for plaster. They plastered over the beams; they created square smooth white rooms as far as possible. Then came the Victorians.

The historical society's MC wears a whistle hanging from his neck. That is the only hint of "organisation".

Towards noon the society turns into a fete champêtre; they couch in groups on the sward, on the banks of the moat, under beech hedge and yew, in orchard and wildery. The talk is of lions passant, harts trippant, of pargetting and spandrels.

A robin sings; then descends from the bough and hops around for a gratuity of crumbs. Ducks come ashore from the moat and organise themselves in a procession.

There is a quiet bustle of packing up. A motorcade streams out of the drive, leaving the old house silent, pleased, a little wistful. "Tick-tock" is the only sound, ticking the years away.

Dancing reeds

November 1975

Ted Ellis

Wordsworth's daffodils, tossing their heads in sprightly dance, were small-time performers compared with Norfolk's graceful reeds, however delightful their setting in the green vistas of Lakeland.

Today, as I looked out to a fringe of marsh where tree-shadows formed a dark back-cloth and sunlight flooded an open area in front, some well-spaced reeds held the stage and displayed their perfect freedom of movement as the wind swirled about them. They looked for all the world like human dancers, swaying, writhing, bowing and thrusting. At times their gestures were those of a group of African braves leaning forward with levelled spears; then they were naiads rising from a pool with tresses flying in an abandon of feminine grace and pale arms pointing to the heavens. They sprang and stood still, like ballet-dancers on tiptoe, assuming classical postures only to pass into the wild whirling of a mêlée of dervishes as an eddy struck them.

There were moments when the stiff leaves streaked out horizontally and trembled or shuddered in a streaming breeze, and sometimes they fluttered like flags in the hand of a signaller, with a military rhythm.

The only music accompanying the reed dancers was their own whispering as they touched crisply in passing, and a faint murmuration of wind in the willows nearby; but the scene conjured up a sweetness of wandering harmonies in the mind: of flutes and panpipes and soft, crooning voices; of drums in the jungle and pibrochs in the hills, while I came to see in every ecstasy of the dances before me a parallel in human grace expressing the freedom of spirit that lies within us all.

Essence of Suffolk – in a word

November 1976

Adrian Bell

Summer's mask is blown away. The leaves dropped from the willows in a night; sprays of ash leaves lie sprawled across the orchard. Giant limbs begin to loom through beech and elm.

A man blew in on the gale to see me, a young man who had been commissioned to write an article on East Anglia. He had been looking round for a week. He felt strongly that it was a peculiarly individual region, like nowhere else in England, but he was baffled to know what was the core of its beautiful difference.

"Perhaps because it is not on the way to anywhere else."

He considered, but that did not satisfy him: there was something much more intrinsic which made it what it was.

"It crumbles into the sea at Aldeburgh, at Dunwich and Lowestoft; and all these are peculiar places in their several ways," I said.

"Lowestoft peculiar?" he queried.

"Why yes: in Lowestoft they marry people in the fish market."

"Some old custom?" I saw his hand feel for his notebook.

"Only as old as since they sited the registrar's office beside the fish quay. On a day in July, what with men bawling fish and rattling ice, my daughter had to ask the registrar to shut the windows so she could hear herself being married."

I switched to asking him about his home life, not wanting to get launched on this subject of Suffolk, which I have been over before, and what there is about it which makes a man like me come for a year and stay for 50.

"Perhaps it's because the towns have no industry to speak of," he suggested.

"No industry?" I exclaimed, and fired at him "Peasenhall,"

"Peasen...?" he began enduringly.

"Peas. Sort of Suffolk double plural, like meezen for mice. For example," I quoted, "They peasen we mew last week wholly want turnin', don't they'll go mowldy."

He looked as though he were trying harder than ever to fathom Suffolk. "I've been to Lavenham," he said.

"Lavenham is a place for visitors to photograph. But for the native, Peasenhall. Because of its drill."

"Drill?" I could see some off-beat physical training centre forming in his mind's eye.

"Corn drill. The peace of mind of innumerable men has depended on the accuracy of Peasenhall's famous corn drill. You should have seen the look in my Walter's eyes as he gripped hold of the steerage, when the going was sticky and the light was bad. You see, that corn has to be drilled as if every green line of it had been ruled with a ruler when it came up. If there was wobble in the rows anywhere, people would stand and peer over the gate and say: "Reckon the chap wot drilled that were walking in his sleep."

"And then there's Long Melford, where a famous Down's TDO plough was manufactured. A draughty place. Walter would say: "The wind blow down Long Melford Street at five o'clock of a February morning fit to cut your liver out."

I felt an eloquent fit about the old days get a grip of me, and tried again to switch the conversation to the young man's family. I poured him a glass of Southwold ale but it brought us back to Suffolk.

"Clare. Clare as noted for its dinners at The Bell kept by Wily Brahma. Also pheasant's-eye corduroy waistcoats."

I told him of the witches of Hundon and the Saints of the Ilketshalls and how a neighbour of mine once had his horse bewitched on the road between Hundon and Cowlinge, so it could not move.

"Are there still witches in Hundon?"

Not since there was an air force station there. To bewitch a bomber would exhaust even a Hundon witch."

" Is that anywhere near Stradishall aerodrome?"

"It was Stradishall aerodrome. They built an aerodrome at Hendon and called it Stradishall. I tell you Suffolk is a peculiar place: it could even make the War Office lose its bearings."

My visitor had been looking at me first with interest, then with patience. Now I thought I caught a trapped look. I glimpsed myself in a wall mirror. Proper windbag you've become, I thought, and stopped.

He got up, said he must be seeing more of Suffolk.

"Didn't there used to be a lot of sheep in Suffolk?" he asked as he climbed into his car.

I bit back the whole subject of Suffolk's folded flocks, and Crabbe's jaundiced view of Aldeburgh sheep and Bloomfield's proud description of West Suffolk sheep. I simply replied: "Yes, there used to be quite a lot of sheep".

Overpage: *A singsong at Fakenham Nursery School.*

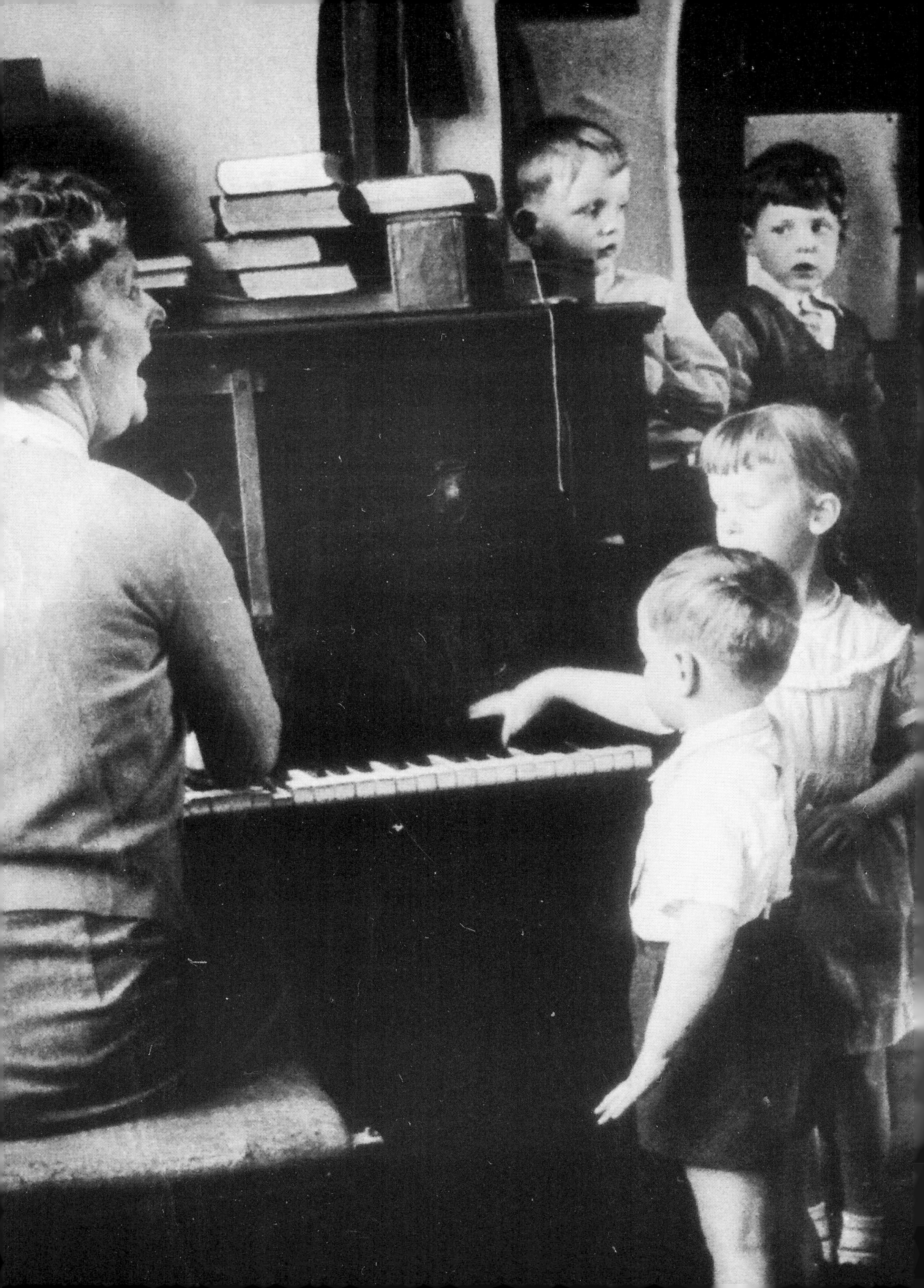

Sculpture in ice

January 1977

Ted Ellis

I never cease to wonder at the endlessly varied forms assumed by the plates of ice which decorate the fringes of our marsh dykes whenever we have a spell of frosty weather.

The magic touch is applied by the rise and fall of the tides, whereby thin sheets of ice are left encrusting emergent reed stems, tree roots, floating mats of litter and driftwood when the water level drops. In the stillness of the night these ice plates develop crystal outgrowths which glitter like all the jewels of fairyland when morning light comes.

Some are like miniature tents of glass, either clear or opaque; many spread like silvery star fishes with webbed arms; there are scintillating fairies'-wand stars with long rays, glittering crescents, moth wing and bat wing shapes, long plumes lying side by side like the pinions of doves or seagulls, and delicate lobes and brackets with fine concentric lines or even bold zebra striping here and there.

In places where there are overhanging trees which contribute drips for part of the day, the encrustations beneath are different again; less frilly and feathery and more polished, rounded and beaded with globules of air. Depending on the height reached by the water on the following tide and on the strength of the frost, the ice sculpture changes from hour to hour and day to day. Sometimes the dykes become completely ice-locked, but even then the crystal growth continues with its fantastic embellishment.

Sand-sculpture

July 1978

Ted Ellis

The rippling of sands on our beaches can be a great source of delight when tides have receded. They are to be seen in wonderful diversity along those parts of the coast where adjacent saltmarshes and underlying beds of clay ensure that water continues to seep and flow down to the sea, often via 'lows' between a succession of sand banks.

The pattern of vein-like channels cut through sloping beaches is similar, in miniature, to that which is typical of deltas in general, but as the streaming lessens towards extreme low tide, great numbers of the temporary watercourses cease their flow altogether and the 'lows' also become mere wet, sandy hollows. It is in the beds of these streamways that one sees the most spectacular undulations of sand-sculpture, involving every conceivable variation in crest and hollow, scalloped by the interacting forces of ebbing waters and irregular flurries of sea breezes.

One day last week, at Brancaster, I kept watch on the flow of runnels as they flowed down beach slopes and was able to see how their sculpting was achieved. Pebbles of various sizes, some of them very small, were scattered over the area and often impeded the flow, sometimes causing diversions, but more usually arresting the progress of the little streams quite briefly. Whenever such an obstruction was encountered, the water level built up to a peak and then curled back in a surging crest. This had the effect of scooping out the bed of the channel just behind the obstruction, loosening its hold, whereupon small stones were then swept forward, coming to rest shortly afterwards in the shallows.

This process was repeated many times, resulting in the carving of channels in a series of ups and downs. Sometimes a puff of wind caused a momentary change of course and this again left its mark in rippled sand. When the tides comes in, all patterns are defaced; but the process starts again with every ebb and each time there is a new display of intricate rippling, whose permutations are infinite.

Magical dawn

June 1979

Ted Ellis

This morning I chanced to rise rather earlier than usual, a little over half-an-hour before dawn, and in the grey of fast fading night, ventured forth into the magical atmosphere of calm and expectancy which is a prelude to all other delights of a summer's day.

There was dew on the grass and a rich fragrance of flowers in the garden. Blackbirds were in full song in the trees about, as were cuckoos further afield, while the cooing of doves had already commenced, wrens uttered staccato trills on awakening and the crowing of a cock pheasant burst explosively from a thicket.

Dozens of pipistrelle bats were just then returning to their roost under the pantiles of an outhouse which they use for a nursery every summer. For a while they circled dizzily at speed as each one awaited its chance to alight and disappear through the one narrow entrance. Bumble bees were already collecting nectar and I found that one loud hum was coming from a queen wasp visiting cotoneaster blossoms at 4am. Small white moths were still dancing round the sweetly scented flowers of a burnet rose and others were visiting the lacy heads of cow parsley where they had shared sweets with mosquitoes on the night.

Presently, as the silvering of marsh vapours cleared with the stirring of a cool little breeze, a golden light suffused the heavens and day had come, by gentle stealth, with the sum beaming upon a green and happy world.

Delights of the Waveney

April 1981

Ted Ellis

The valley of the river Waveney, which divides Norfolk from Suffolk, is for the greater part wide and green with water meadows. The woods and thickets on its flanks harbour nightingales in summer, where sunny slopes once favoured the development of vineyards and even now are a refuge of several rare wild flowers which are absent farther north, while at its source is a superb fen, the only remaining British haunt of the large swamp spider *(Dolomedes plantarius)*.

The river itself is the least polluted of those flowing into the Broads system and in winter its upper reaches are subject to spectacular flooding whenever there are heavy rains.

On the day our first swallow came home and morning mist gave way to sunshine, I went down to the Waveney at Ellingham Mill, in the knowledge that it would provide special delights in the warmth and glow of early spring at daffodil time. The white-boarded mill is now an art gallery nestling among the splendour of colourful and fragrant flower beds.

Nearby, the river and adjacent mill stream tumble over a series of weirs, large and small, offering a sparkling vista of waterfalls, large and small. I found evidence of the past winter's high water levels in great wisps of flood debris caught up and held in the branches of riverside willows and other trees; but now, although the flow was still generous, there were sandy shoals and duck-haunted islands just below the influx cascading from the weirs.

In this area the river was teeming with thousands of dace heading aggressively upstream. The fish were concentrated under the largest weir and many were attempting to scale the sloping concrete platforms where waters raced and foamed. They were behaving like salmon, flashing silver as they leapt and struggled forward. At times they seemed to scurry along like mice where the water was shallow in one particular place, but where a fierce, boiling current held sway, they became visible only as they darted from the foam briefly, only to be hurled back.

Dace are commonly present in trout streams where there is plenty of movement in the water, but I have never before seen them leaping at waterfalls.

Theatre Royal

Central Library blaze

August 1994

Charles Roberts

Even as the reality began to sink in, there remains a sense of deep shock, of sick disbelief, at what happened.

The loss of a fine lending library, disastrous as it is, one can handle – it is largely replaceable.

The real and numbing catastrophe is that what has been wrenched from us in a few hours is an irreplaceable tapestry in print of centuries of Norfolk and Norwich life.

Gone are the Rye, Colman and American Memorial libraries and the entire and richly distinctive local studies section which brought enlightenment, pleasure and the excitement of discovery to countless thousands of us.

Walter Rye, eccentric, antiquarian and generous benefactor, devoted his time and money to "tracing the minutest points of historical importance" of Norfolk and Norwich, as the city librarian wrote at the time of his death 65 years ago.

The vast collection of books and material he left to the city and which was added to over the years, was thus based on small things through which came the voices of ordinary people from our shared past, and of events both great and small in a chequered history...

They were voices heard through playbills and ephemera, in little chapbooks from the 18th century, like the enchanting illustrated one which told the story of Tom Hickathrift, the legendary Marshlands giant.

Here too were innumerable local books, some entirely irreplaceable, others only at huge expense. Here were maps and prints and old photographs, opening for us sepia windows on to epochs long gone.

And here, too, an enthusiast for Norfolk's wonderful churches might borrow from a mighty collection of 2000 slides.

Two weeks ago, as I have done on numerous occasions over the years, I borrowed 50 of them to augment my own collection for a lecture – and didn't get around to returning them last week.

Yesterday I was due to drop in at lunchtime to take them back...

The delight of local studies was that the enthusiasm of the inquirer was matched by the enthusiasm, helpfulness and knowledge of the staff.

As when I set out to discover just why St James the Great was recognised by the symbol of a scallop shell... Several barrow loads of dusty tomes were brought down from the stack – the tall block at the back of the building – before the answer to my quest was dicovered. And no one was happier than my helper.

A few books from the ground floor level are retrievable, though damaged. In the back of the building several boxes of Press cuttings have survived. Some books from the original Norwich library, which flourished from 1608 for a couple of hundred years, have come through, smoke-blackened but restorable.

But all else, from the ground floor upwards, has perished.

"Virtual devastation," the chief fire officer called it. I met the county's head of libraries, Hilary Hammond, moments after he had emerged from the still-smouldering remains.

It was no surprise that he was grey with shock. But the sickening impact of what was happening had hit him much earlier. As he was driving into Norwich he saw the great column of smoke hanging with uneerie stillness over the city, switched on his car radio and heard that the flagship library of his county service was ablaze.

As both he and Jean Kennedy, head of the Records Office, admitted yesterday, the total shock had still to hit them. But for Miss Kennedy at least there is a palpable atom of comfort in which we can all share.

Her department, housed underground against just such a catastrophe, contains the unique manuscript material which carries the story of city and county back 900 years. It is all intact! Water damaged, yes.

This below-ground department was designed as the last redoubt, so whatever happened, the records would go last. Within its care were county records going back to the 16th century; the ancient records of Norwich, Yarmouth, the Diocese and Dean and Chapter of Norwich, of 650 of the 700 parishes in Norfolk, family and estate manuscript collections and medieval manuscript maps.

Something, at least, for which to be grateful on this dark day in our county town's 800th anniversary charter year.

Queen of Hearts

April 1996

Charles Roberts

Pomp, pageantry and splendour melded with essential simplicity and very human emotion yesterday when Norwich Cathedral was the setting for the first time in its 900-year span for the Royal Maundy service. For more than an hour before the Queen and the Duke of Edinburgh made their ceremonial entry through the Great West Door, the cathedral had been quietly filling with a congregation which, appropriately on this day of ancient Christian significance, embraced the very young to the venerably old, and brought together a broad span of the county's life.

It was a morning of clear skies and intense wintery sunlight which streamed in through the south triforium and lit up the Caen stone of the thrusting Norman nave, turning the stone to honeyed mellowness where the light struck, and paling to pearl grey under the arches of the north clerestory.

As we waited, Bishop Lyhart's mighty 15th century vaulted roof itself became matter for contemplation, for it puts into context a ceremony even as old as Maundy Thursday, upon which Saint Augustine commented nigh on 1400 years ago. For the carved bosses which lock the vaults tell a story stretching from Creation to the Ascension... with a final bay of examples and warnings to weak and mortal men.

As the Duke of Edinburgh was to read in the first lesson, Jesus washed his disciples' feet and gave them a new commandment, or mandatum (thus Maundy): "I have given you an example, that ye should do as I have done to you".

The Queen, as is well known, has taken this text to heart and made the Royal Maundy service a special feature of her reign. In stepping down from her exalted place near the High Altar to walk around the cathedral to hand out the Maundy purses to those who had given their time and commitment to community and Church, she is re-enacting the humility, compassion, service and example established 2000 years ago in Jerusalem.

By now time was passing. Cued precisely on time (an immensely impressive element of every part of the service and ceremony which were to follow) the first procession moved down the first aisle – the ecumenical procession symbolising the brotherhood, if not the unity, of Christian Churches – Roman Catholic, Free Churches, Salvation Army, Quakers.

Then the Rural Deans and Archdeacons of the Norwich Diocese, the Diocesan Registrar and the Chancellor, grave in his full-bottomed wig.

Minutes pass, filled by the swirling notes of the organ high on its screen. Now comes the cathedral procession, led by the cathedral mace, its bearer with a face as graven and serene as a carved image. Immediately behind him, taking part in perhaps its greatest ceremonial since its creation, the girls' choir of the cathedral, 22 young ladies with a contained dignity beyond their years.

Their madonna-blue robes contrast with the regal gold, scarlet and black tabards of The Children of the Chapel Royal who follow in their wake, small boys conscious of their role and reflecting it in the intensity of their faces and the precision of their martial

tread. Gentlemen of the Chapel Royal, the cathedral choir, clergy and canons move after them, their plain cassocks and surplices touched by the varied colours of their academic hoods.

Now the Great West Doors swing open, and more sunlight streams in and glints on the cross and candles which herald the procession of rich colour and panoply up the centre aisle: the suffragan Bishops of Thetford and Lynn, the Dean and Vice dean, superbly vested in richly crafted copes; the bewigged Chapter Clerk, and the imposing presence of The High Steward, Earl Ferrers.

Moments later, moving in the opposite direction up the south aisle, the click upon the flagged floor of the stick carried by the Sergeant Major of the Gentlemen of the Yeomen of the Guard (please don't call them Beefeaters, who are the Yeomen Warders of the Tower) announces the Yeomen who will join up at the West Door with the procession of the Lord High Almoner – the ancient office which for centuries has looked after the Sovereign's charities and responsibilities towards the poor.

The pageantry is growing now, the sense of anticipation increasing. The Almoner, Sub Almoner and their officials wear, thrown over their shoulders and wound round their waists, linen towels to represent those which in former times were used by the Sovereign and attendants to wash the feet of the folk who would receive the Maundy bounty.

In their midst are the Children of the Royal Almonry – four specially chosen children carrying the traditional posies which in times past were thought to ward off disease – and certainly helped ward off the evil smells which assailed royal and noble nostrils.

Throughout this time the organ has been issuing quiet voluntaries. But suddenly it has swelled to pealing and thundering and celebratory fanfares. For at the door are the Sovereign and the Duke, who enter with the Queen's Suite and the Bishop of Norwich, and three Gentlemen Yeomen bearing on their heads silver gilt dishes (brought specially from the repository of the Crown Jewels) bearing the Maundy purses which soon will be distributed.

As they move down the centre aisle, the congregation launches into the hymn, Praise to the Holiest in the Height. The long awaited service has begun.

Her Majesty, glowing in a coat and hat of springtime coral pink, looks happy, relaxed and smiling and far younger than her 70 years. She moves through to the presbytery at the east end, to sit feet away from where her predecessor in name, Elizabeth I, sat 418 years ago.

Twice during the service Her Majesty progresses down through the cathedral, first on the south side, then on the north, to hand the Maundy purses to 70 men and 70 women, representing her age. Meanwhile, from beyond the organ screen, anthems soar joyfully from the combined choirs of Chapel Royal and Cathedral.

As the Queen moves down the north aisle the organ is rumbling out the tensioned introductory bars of Handle's great coronation anthem, Zadok the Priest.

At the very moment that Her Majesty turns into the centre aisle, in front of the West Doors, the exhilarating opening words of the anthem burst from the choirs in a blaze of sound, a moment of wonderful coincidence which intensifies the extraordinary atmosphere of the memorable service.

From the trays carried by the Yeomen, the purses are handed by Almoner and Sub-Almoner into the Sovereign's hands, and she in turn, smiling and at ease, gives them to the recipients, the pleasure on whose faces is a joy in itself to see.

One elderly gentleman is so overwhelmed by the moment that he holds out his hands as if to receive the Host. The Queen does not simply give him the purses, but briefly takes his hand as the transfer takes place. He glows, smiles and bows in sheer delight.

All those present yesterday will not forget the splendour of the occasion. But it is little cameos like that just described which will forever mark Maundy Thursday in this 900th year of Norwich Cathedral & Diocese.

Her Majesty tours the Cathedral after the Royal Maundy service.

Her Majesty The Queen at the Royal Maundy service at Norwich Cathedral in 1996. It was the first time in its 900-year history that the Cathedral has hosted the event.

The Norwich to Sheringham line

November 1996

Charles Roberts

Clack and rattle of wheels over points. Comforting sway of railway carriage. Only the thud of diesel to remind us that steam has simmered into history.

The countryside is cold, bleak, battened down under arctic winds, the trees starved into charcoal.

North Norfolk in November – yet still with a landscape magic as appealing in its way as basking summer and cirrus-scudding skies.

The 09.52 from Norwich to Sheringham is safely on its way, steadily drumming through settlements and countryside moulded by the hands of builders and farmers through a thousand years – a panorama fixed and dated from Saxon church towers to unstoppable rashes of modern development.

Norwich Thorpe Station on this morning of bitter cold is a frigid wind tunnel. I grab a mug of hot chocolate and a sustaining chocolate bar and head for platform 5b where warmth in the "John Constable" awaits me... just one little unit, hardly longer than a hissing 2-4-0 in the East Norfolk Railway's golden days.

"Dick and Dorothea Callum had never been in Norfolk before, and for ten minutes they had been waiting in (Thorpe) *station, sitting in the train for fear it should go again at once, as it had at Ipswich...."*

Thus we enter the opening page of Arthur Ransome's 1934 children's classic, Coot Club... an echo of those railway days when London into the heart of Norfolk and on to the coast was a straight-through ride.

But let's not complain, for The Cromer Branch, as the Norwich-Sheringham line was known in the steam era, is now vested in Anglia Railways, in an arrangement which safeguards it for at least seven years. Hooray for that!

Close the book on Dick and Dorothea's summer journey, Wroxham-bound. Back to November '96. Out through Thorpe, smoothing beside the River Yare, choppy, chilled and deserted save for occasional coots, bobbing like rubber ducks on a bath, and a single grebe, cresting through the water like a full-rigged brigantine off Biscay.

Below us the diesel motors deepen to bass as we climb steadily. Countryside opens to the right. To the left, a solid swathe of new suburban development, red bricks and tiles as raw and unmellowed as the morning.

About here it was, on the fateful night of September 10, 1874, that human error precipitated an horrendous accident, as two trains upon the same line thundered towards each other through the night.

They collided "with a fearful velocity", as the Yarmouth Independent was to describe it, "the terrible force of the collision causing in a moment of time a scene of wreck and ruin such as has seldom been witnessed".

To the right, a vast ploughed field, drear and waterlogged as trenches on the Somme, before Salhouse station slides by, affording a brief glimpse of its Victorian platform canopies on their twirly cast-iron spandrels – touches we'll see often on this line, of a character to please the heart of Mr Betjeman.

Clattering wheel song heralds the descent towards Wroxham, as suburbia embraces the line in a tunnelled hug. A brief glimpse of the Bure and herring-bone ranks of boats, wrapped and tied for winter like parcels bound for distant shores.

On again, past clapboard signal box, new when Lord Suffield ruled the East Norfolk line. Past great fields, neatly hedged, framing winter corn green as springtime and ploughed acres of glacial chocolate, under a sky as grey as frostbite.

Off to the right, a distant glimpse in a shield of trees, a great church tower of cold flint splendour and a flash of soaring Perpendicular windows. Tunstead, I think. Then a smaller, homelier church to the left, a quiet motet of flint, under thatched roof and festooned with scaffolding – could it be Sloley, guardian of one of the most exhilaratingly carved medieval fonts in the county?

Worstead station passes in a blink. More Betjemanesque cast iron and canopies, but winter has erased the station's colourful summer glory of flowers. Past the village's mighty "wool" church beyond... shades of William Paston, six hundred years ago, writing to his cousin Robert: "I shall make my doublet all worstead, for the glory of Norfolk".

To the left, a forest of wind-flurried firs stands black as a Chinese frieze. To the right the landscape changes, undulating, wooded, only to change in a moment as another rash of raw new houses announces the spreading outskirts of North Walsham... into whose station the train slides, smooth and crafty as a cat.

We stand several minutes at the platform, the electric doors wide open, inviting in a hard-edged wedge of polar wind. "Norfolk Motor Cycle Museum", says a sign to the right. A new one for me. Beside it, a desolate old railway building lies shattered and abandoned, emblem of changing times and needs.

We move on, the eye drawn by the great craggy, fallen cliff of North Walsham's church tower, which young Nelson would have known, for it sundered a good half century before he began his grammar school days in the town.

Out of Walsham now, bungalows to the right of us, bungalows to the left of us, but no volley and thunder on this morning of dull steel.

Into undulating, comfortable, wooded country the line eases, the view punctuated by the flinted fingers of church towers which characterise the whole of this county of Norfolk. Far off to the left, encircled by woodland is a tower of another kind. A Chinese pagoda? No, it's the clock tower of Gunton Hall, seat of that great 19th century magnate Lord Suffield, chairman of the East Norfolk Railway.

His Lordship did fairly well out of it. Much of the land for the new railway belonged to him. And from his estate came most of the ballast and brick-clay. All grist to m'lord's mill - he had one of those too, state of the art, adding yet more to his bank balance.

Later Gunton would have another claim to fame. The Prince of Wales, the future King Edward VII, rented it on a regular basis for months at a time. The rental included the little dower house, Elderton Lodge... and there Miss Lily Langtree and other favoured pretty ladies would be billeted, awaiting calls to the hall for imperial duties and thoughts of England.

So when we see Gunton Station from the train we know why it's so grand, with its solid brick building (now a private house), with smart hipped roof and a splendidly elegant canopy over the platform to greet his Lordship and his guests – and those of the potent prince.

Into a series of cuttings. Out to etched trees against the sky. Off to the right, another church but a very special one: Southrepps, its tower elegant as starched Tudor collars and redeeming lace and one of the best in all Norfolk.

Trees close in on what is now a single line. As we pass over a rural bridge, a woman below walks her labradors, one sand, one black, she as enveloped in her winter warmers as they in their fluffed-out furs.

And so to the sea, heralded by thrusting little hills bristling with gorse and ragged trees. The line swings in a great arc, taking us inevitable as gravitational pull into Cromer Beach, where Benbow's Farm Shop, Safeways, b&b, brave new apartment blocks and fancy-bricked houses by the score engulf this station cul-de-sac.

Away again, in reverse, past West Runton's little church, perched on a knoll betwixt railway and sea – and hemmed in by vistas of caravans, tight packed and anchored and dreaming of the open road.

A couple of decades back the BBC made a film about John Betjeman on the King's Lynn-Hunstanton line, he in his eccentric hat and old coat and carrying the inevitable shopping bag. Days after it was screened the Beeb received a call from the police: An old gentleman in a large hat and old coat and carrying a string bag had been seen wandering along the line at West Runton – could it be Mr Betjeman?

The BBC was able to reassure the caller that Mr B was safe in London, tucked up at home... his doppelgänger remained unidentified.

So to Sheringham and the end of the line, where the wind is lethal as claws and abrasive as sea salt. Winter ozone cleaves through the streets, triumphantly keening its achievement in driving every palpable pong of chip fat, fish fry and sick-sweet candy floss scent out to the wallowing ocean.

But there'll be another summer, another holiday invasion. And for the next seven years at least, they can come by train, that transport of delight, occasion and adventure that the automobile can never equal.

Strange noises in the shadows

January 1997

Charles Roberts

Wild creatures, I sometimes think, have a psychic contact with us and our doings. Though such is the way of the wild that it is but a one-way reaching-out.

A dear friend in North Norfolk, one who had loved the locality's open skies and marshes and birds and the overall richness of its natural life, was being buried. As – dust to dust, ashes to ashes – she was lowered into God's good earth, a skein of wild geese arrowed overhead, voicing a mournful salute.

Was it more a salute to life and continuance, rather than to a sad passing, that a few days ago, as volunteers laboured at Hickling Broad to do their bit in rebuilding habitats for Norfolk's rarest bird, a bittern forsook its shadowed, secretive ways and flew, clear against the sky, over their heads?

These birds are members of a very exclusive club – they are among the rarest and most endangered breeding species in Britain. Just 22 males survive in these islands, 16 of them in Norfolk and Suffolk.

Near 40 years ago, when first I discovered the Broads, the whole area was alive with bitterns. Not that I'd even heard the word bittern then. Born and brought up in the countryside of the Midlands, I knew my coots and moorhens and grebes. But not the boomer of the marshes. That, however, was to be put right on a night never to be forgotten.

To Norfolk a half dozen of us had come, a quartet of 16-year-olds and a couple of youngsters, mere 14-year-olds, keenly excited at the prospect of collecting our cruiser and (visions of Rattie and Wind in the Willows and messing about in boats) embarking on a week-long Broads holiday.

Our travels brought us one evening to the River Ant, that lonely waterway which winds and serpentines through marshland and sedge.

We chose a spot to moor for the night. Not a dwelling, not even a windmill in sight, and the river that late afternoon wholly deserted. "Can we take out the rowing boat?" asked the "youngsters". They were granted leave – as long as they didn't go far.

We four elders, left to ourselves, settled down to tea and talk of our week's adventures and the content of the day's log. Oh, we did things properly then. And guess who wrote the log!

Time passed. Suddenly: "Hey, there's not a sound out there. Wonder where the boys are."

We hurried up "on deck". The light was beginning to pale. There was a hint of mist. A slight wind moaned under its breath. The reeds took up its chorus. But of rowing boat and youngsters there was neither sight nor sound.

Fifteen minutes passed. Twenty. Thirty. Twilight was on the edge of darkness, that indeterminate interlude which the French eerily call *l'heure entre chien et loup* – the hour between dog and wolf.

"Two of you go down the bank that way, we'll go in the opposite direction," said one, taking command (he was, it goes without saying, a senior prefect at his public school).

We went, continuing until we could barely see, then stumbled back to the boat. No luck from the other two either. We were worried now, seriously worried – four teenagers faced with a man-size fear.

Around us the marshes had become hostile territory. Things moved and rustled and slithered. The lap and suck of water at bank and keel was predatory now. The previously confident foursome were now increasingly nervous.

It was then that we heard it, like something from a bad dream or a Boy's Own tale of travels in faraway lands. A strange, chilling, booming sound which came from everywhere and nowhere, which chilled our blood and made our hair stand on end...

The sound faded, stopped, and we looked at each other, pale in the half light. It was at that very moment that another sound eased over the Ant's dark waters – the unmistakable, reassuring thud and splash of oars. The boys had come home.

There was a row, of course, a big one. Like parents, we covered up our intense relief with inflated fury.

We did not have a good night at our mooring. All were ill at ease, sleeping badly. There was something wrong about this spot...

Next morning, we bought a large boating map of the river. There, looking up at us, was the name of the river stretch where we'd passed the dark hours: Skeleton's Reach!

Previous pages: *The Tinkler family of Norwich play cricket on the beach at Hemsby in the early 1960s.*

Biographies

Lilias Rider Haggard

Lilias Rider Haggard – daughter of Sir Henry, author of King Solomon's Mines – wrote for seven years up to December 1942 a weekly column for the Eastern Daily Press called The Country Woman's Week. Afterwards she continued to have articles published in the paper. Henry Williamson called her pieces "the best thing of its kind in contemporary journalism". She served in the Nursing Auxiliaries during the first world war, and was awarded the MBE in 1919. Three collections of her EDP work were published; Norfolk Life, A Norfolk Notebook and A County Scrapbook. Born 1892; died 1968.

Henry Williamson

Henry Williamson came to Norfolk from Devon, where he had written Tarka the Otter. He farmed at Old Hall Farm, Stiffkey for seven years and was a regular contributor to the Eastern Daily Press. A collection of his articles, entitled Green Fields and Pavements: A Norfolk Farmer in Wartime, was published in 1995 by the Henry Williamson Society. Williamson fought in the first world war and was involved in the Christmas Truce, when soldiers from both sides swapped rations and played football together. Born 1895; died 1977.

Eric Fowler

Eric Fowler, a member of the EDP staff, became a much loved institution as Jonathan Mardle. He joined Eastern Counties Newspapers in 1925, and created the Mardle pseudonym in 1946, writing the column up to and beyond his retirement from the company in 1974. He was awarded the MBE in 1968. At his memorial service at Norwich Cathedral in January 1982, the Dean of Gloucester said of him: "As a writer he had the power to make history and to become a part of history so that in centuries to come wise folk will rediscover us with him." Born 1909; died 1981.

Adrian Bell

Author, journalist and farmer, Adrian Bell wrote the Countryman's Notebook in the Eastern Daily Press for thirty years, from 1949. Among his books are the rural trilogy Corduroy, The Cherry Tree and Silver Ley. In February 1930 he compiled the first Times crossword, and nursed his creation for many years. He described this work as "the ideal job for a chap with a vacant mind, sitting on a tractor harrowing clods, or bicycling." He was a romantic, though a thoroughly practical one, and a countryman to the heart whose writings, as the EDP said at his death, "raised the craft of the essayist to its highest level." Born 1901; died 1980.

Ted Ellis

Most people will remember Ted Ellis' newspaper work from the initials E.A.E at the bottom of the In The Countryside series that he began in the Eastern Daily Press in 1946. His work also included radio and television. Rosemary Tilbrook, who now contributes to the In The Countryside column, said of Ted: "We all live in 'our county' of Norfolk. But he, in a remote cottage at Wheatfen Broad among 130 acres of beloved wilderness... 'was Norfolk.'" Born 1909; died 1986.

Ralph Mottram

Author of The Spanish Farm, one of the major novels about the Great War and based on his own experiences, Ralph Mottram dedicated his life to Norwich through public service and writing. He wrote more than sixty books, and was Lord Mayor of the city in Coronation Year, 1953-54. Born 1883; died 1971.

Clifford Butler

Clifford Butler was for twenty years the editor of the Norwich Mercury Series of weekly newspapers, sister papers to the Eastern Daily Press. Born 1920; died 1981.

Charles Roberts

Charles Roberts is Arts Editor of the Eastern Daily Press, and writes a weekly column for the newspaper. He came to Norfolk twenty eight years ago, intending to stay six months. He is deeply involved in the life of the county, and has a passion for the protection of its heritage and landscape.